CW00741088

HOW THE IRISH SPEAK ENGLISH

How the Irish speak English

Padraic O'Farrell

MERCIER PRESS

Mercier Press Limited
P.O. Box 5, 5 French Church Street, Cork *and*
24 Lower Abbey Street, Dublin 1

© Padraic O'Farrell, 1980, 1993

First published 1980
Revised edition 1993

ISBN 1-85635-055-X

A CIP catalogue record for this book
is available from the British Library

To 'The world and his wife'

Printed in Ireland by Colour Books Ltd.

Contents

Acknowledgements

My wife, Maureen, took a particular interest in this book and she diligently noted down many gems that dropped from the lips of strangers as I engaged them in conversation. 'May you be in Heaven an hour before the devil knows you're dead, love!'

'Is this a good saying, Da?' – that was the question most asked by Declan, Noel, Niamh and Aisling as they related some new phrase heard that day. I thank them all for their help. Annette O'Dowd was the staff member of Longford/Westmeath library who 'took the heavy end of the stick' acquiring books. I thank the following who gave tremendous help in passing on material: Mai Savage, Joe McPartland, Comdt Pat McKevitt, James Lyons, Andy Dowling, Sister Attracta, John Louis Coleman, Joe McGarrigle, Jervis King, Sister Concilio, Sean McEvoy, Dinny McMahon, the Vaughan brothers and Jack Higgins.

Foreword

Descriptive phrases etching
Blueprints for kindred structures
In responsive recesses;
Fashioning designs.
Come ambassadors,
Furnishing flesh and features
On their imagery;
Replacing it with memories
For the future.
Memories –
And blessings.

The reader may well ask what that amateurish flight to the antechamber of the Muses has to do with a book of sayings and expressions of the Irish people. Let me explain.

There are thousands of Irish-Americans who have never been to this country and who attempt to visualise their relations here. After years of planning and hoping, for they have a great wish to know more about our land and our people, they eventually make a visit and meet their uncles and cousins and perhaps their grandparents.

I penned those lines after such a visit. A cousin and her daughter.

They saw places and met people. They talked – and they *listened*. We spoke to them with difficulty, for after we'd said something which to us was quite normal, Joan, the mother, would instruct her daughter, Maureen, to write it down. We had to repeat it. It had to be written accurately and often phonetically, for what intrigued our guests were our sayings and expressions.

It was then that I realised that these phrases were worth recording, and so I set about a task that took me to many corners of the country to meet hundreds of people, and was to put me in contact with as many more.

My book does not set out to educate but to entertain. It is not a study of intricacies of dialect – many fine works by scholarly people are available on that subject. Neither does it claim to be a comprehensive collection of derivatives of our mother tongue.

No. My book merely offers a selection of common words, sayings and expressions of the Irish people. Some are old, some are new, some are plain and some are witty.

I felt that a mere tabulation of these sayings and expressions with their explanations would tend to become monotonous, and so I attempted to present them within a loose narrative, leavened with a few anecdotes. They are associated, in the book, with the counties from which they came. It is important to realise, however, that ours is a small island and that many of our people move from the county of their birth to set their roots elsewhere.

For this reason, sayings and expressions heard in a particular county may well have had their origins elsewhere. They may also vary slightly in construction from place to place. Come with me then, and 'speak' this book instead of reading it, for it is intonation, emphasis and accent that give our sayings and expressions their true charm.

Padraic O'Farrell

Leinster

ALMOST IN the dead centre of Ireland is the village of Bally-more, described by a visitor as a 'town with no middle and two inds' because of its topography. I choose this spot to begin my chapter on Leinster sayings because of the legend associated with the place which was once a de Lacey stronghold and where, in 1648, Eoghan Roe O'Neill defeated an Ormondist force while leading his Ulster warriors to relieve Athy.

The town of Ballymore was once situated north of its present position, and it boasted a fine spring well. A big stone in the well was useful for standing upon to fill pails of water. There was one woman of the 'Paddy-go-aisy' type who used to stand on this stone and wash her linen in the well and pound the garments on the stone with her wash-staff.

This angered more than the villagers, for one day water began spouting from the ground all around her. It drowned her and flooded an area of eighty acres or so, and is still there, bearing the name of Lough Seudy.

I use this as an introduction because Leinster has been flooded with migrants from other parts of Ireland, and so, either by right or adoption, has acquired a wealth of sayings and expressions. These people who come to live in the industrial areas surrounding our capital are 'runners'. They are welcome in these areas because they are useful to the economy. They may even be liked – unless they step out of line and take on something that ought to be reserved for a native of the soil. They are seldom wholly accepted. Christian Ireland, 'you're rearin' them yet' – the 'begrudgers', 'aginers', who forget that the 'spalpeen' was once a respectable wandering labourer.

The Wicklow Goat Suckers are a divided people with a great mountain range running through their territory and with every inch of every heathery field steeped in lore: Michael Dwyer leading his pursuers a merry dance around Imaal, his young wife ogling a yeoman to his death, and the Slaney beginning its meandering course which takes it through '98 country.

'I'll make you cough up thrupenny bits,' threatens a Wicklow mother.

A father uses a stronger, 'I'll kick you into the middle of next week'.

'You're getting as big as a house.'

'I wouldn't work for him if I was paid.'
'There's no standing that fellow.'
'I'm destroyed walking.'
'He ran like a redshank' or 'like a mountain goat'.

The two closest towns in Ireland are Arklow and Gorey because there's only an Inch between them. Arklow has its rich sea folklore, and old customs are still observed there. Give a wrong answer to an Arklowman and he will say, 'You're as far out as the lighthouse'. Give him plenty of cigarettes during a chat and he will say of you the next day, 'He was handing them around like snuff at a wake'.

A cow is let out on the side of the road to graze 'God's acre' and a decent Wicklow farmer 'would give you his last penny'.

'As crooked as a ram's horn.'
'As sweet as a whistle.'
'He knows no more about it than a pig does about an armchair.'
'That one has a bee in her bonnet about something.'
'Talk away – your tongue is no scandal', is directed at

someone who is a chatterbox and therefore will not be listened to or heeded.

'That fellow didn't come down in the last shower' – he is cute.

'He went along to them, cap in hand'; 'He went touching the forelock to them' – he was servile. 'He went with his finger in his gob', however, means that he went without knowing what he was looking for.

'You're on the pig's back' means you are made up.

In Aughavanna one night, I heard a singer falter while performing. He used a saying that I had only read before. It originated in the days when ballad sheets were sold: 'There's a hole in the ballad.'

But hurry, Fr Murphy from old Kilcormack is 'spurring' up the rocks with a warning cry, that if we don't 'get to hell' down to Wexford quickly, he'll 'put his ten commandments on our faces'. This expression is more often used of a girl, and it means putting the marks of ten fingernails down one's face, or 'scraubing'.

You'd want to be up early in the morning to catch out a Wexfordman, God love them, the Wexford people take to the stranger 'like a calf to the teat'. Even if one of them had 'bugger-all to give you' he would 'take off like a cat with a fryin' pan tied to its arse' to get you something. An odd one of them is 'as cross as a two-ended briar'. He would be called 'an old *sceach*'. The 'two-ended briar' has a place in Wicklow folk-lore where it is said that passing under one and requesting the Devil to do a favour brings results.

A pompous Wexfordman: 'He had a head on him like Blackwater.'

Caught out in the rain, a woman 'is dreepin'', as she sticks her head in a neighbour's door and says, 'Here's me head and the rest of me is comin''. She might be 'as thin as a whippet' and 'as flat as a pancake', but 'be the livin' jinnets' she's 'as good an old skin as ever wore shoe-leather'.

The offhand nature of Wexford people gave rise to two peculiar sayings during the Second World War. Scarce commodities were passed around then and great thanks would be bestowed for the gift of an ounce or two of tea. The donor would shrug off the kind deed by saying, 'Ah thank your mother for the rabbits, the soup was lovely!' It was a long-winded, 'Ah, for nothing!' 'How's your mother for sugar?' earned the reply, 'Up to her eyes in tea' – a sarcastic declaration that she had neither sugar nor tea. A farmer paid his labourer '£5 a week and dietem'; he 'gave him his keep as well as paying him'; he 'dieted' him.

'A quare fine day.'
'It was a quare good game.'
'He was a strong farmer' – he had a big farm.
'Shraums' was matter running from the eyes.
A 'pusthaghaun' was a conceited person.
A 'molly' was a sissy, an effeminate male.
A 'laudydaw' was a stuck-up or very grand person.
'She went hot-foot after him!'

A 'gripe' is a ditch, 'grawls' are children, and a 'grape' is a four-pronged fork.

If a couple are 'mighty coonagh', they are 'going strong', or 'walking out'. If they are 'chawing the rag', they are continually bickering.

Little used now is the term 'buannaioch' for the last sheaf of corn which custom demanded should be bound by a girl if she wished to remain unmarried.

The ambition of any true Wexfordman should be;

> To smoke his dudheen (pipe with no shank);
> To drink his cruiskeen (jug of liquor);
> To wave his alpeen (stick);
> To wallop his spalpeen (labourer)

– and before he does, let me 'lep' across the Blackstairs and do battle with the Kilkenny Cats.

> *It brought me back my own sweet Nore,*
> *The castle and the Mill;*
> *Until my eyes could see no more,*
> *The moon behind the hill.*

There are few finer sights in this fair land than the impressive Butler castle in the town of St Cainneach or Canice – except, perhaps, St Canice's cathedral and round tower themselves.

A county famous for its hurlers, there is a quiet confidence among its people. You 'wouldn't call the King your uncle' if you were a Kilkennyman. They will play hard, strike hard, but are 'the soul of decency' behind it all. They criticise a bad hurler by saying: 'He is like a lighthouse in a bog – brilliant but useless.' If you asked them, 'Where's the back?' in a pub (seeking the toilet), they might tell you, or they might say you were 'as ignorant as a kish (basket) of brogues (boots)' – or, more simply, 'as thick as a stone wall'.

If a person has no sense, they say: 'He hasn't a titter of wit', 'He can't see beyond his nose', or 'He hasn't the brains of a sparrow'.

A mean Kilkennyman is 'afraid to sneeze in case he'd give anything away'. As the song says:

> *We'll smoke our own*
> *And drink our own*
> *In dacent Tullaroan*

'She thinks she's the bees' knees and the spiders' ankles' is the slightly envious comment on a well-dressed lady. A kindly Ballyragget nun gave me a description of a lady in high heels – 'She was like a cat on a scissors.'

Have they a pessimistic attitude to love by the Nore? Of a love-affair that blossoms, they say, 'Oh, the first soup is always the hottest'. When one appears in his true colours, they say, 'That's the porridge breaking out in the soup'.

'He was throwing the sprat but the salmon wasn't biting.'

'He knows as much about religion as a pig does about a clean shirt.'

A cute fellow is 'fattening pigs in another man's garden', and the arch robber would 'steal the eye out of your head and come back for the eyelashes'.

'As stout as the back of a ditch.'

'I gave him a piece of my mind' – I told him off.

'He'd build a nest in your ear.'

'They weren't gushy about it' – they didn't enthuse.

'I'll make him scratch where he doesn't itch' – I'll punish him in some way.

'She had a mug of consequence on her' – she had notions about herself; she thought she was 'it'.

'He's as odd as two left feet.'

'May you never have a blind child but you'll have a lame one to lead it.'

The Midlands

The Carlow 'Scallion-Eaters', Kildare 'Lily Whites' and the people of Laois, Offaly, Westmeath and Longford comprise, for the purpose of this book at least, the inhabitants of the Midlands. Flat, rolling pastureland that includes the finest beef-fattening land in the world survives a 'stone's throw' from the great Bog of Allen. The derisive term, 'bogman', got a 'quick shift' during the war when well-dressed city men picked their careful way through muddy boreens to do a deal with a turf-cutter who would keep their factories or hotels heated until the foreign coal came back to our shores.

> *A whistling woman and a crowing hen*
> *Will make a man wealthy but the dear knows when.*

Whistling Carlow women were obviously a rarity when these old lines were penned.

A request for money that only receives a little response is accompanied by the remark, 'That's all I've threshed'. 'Trams', which are the rear shafts of carts elsewhere, are haycocks in Carlow as well as further afield. A Carlow woman always kept a 'thrashbag' – a long series of bags full of buttons, threads and other household accoutrements.

'I felt like shutting the terr in the tauloge.' The speaker thought of locking an annoying '*cábóg*' of a fellow in a recess by the hearth where brushes and things are stored.

'Snazzy' has replaced 'snish' in describing a neatly dressed fellow. If his father was a neat dresser too, 'His nibs didn't catch it in the wind'.

'Better than' means 'more than' in Carlow. 'I got better than I asked for.' If the donor made a compliment of so giving, he would be told, 'Ah, don't be making so much bones about it' – a modern version is 'stick it up your jumper', or a place lower and less accessible! 'Cadging' or being 'on the cadge' is scrounging. A 'cleg' is a horsefly, and 'dido' is a dressed-up girl. If she were not all there, she would be a 'googeen'. A similar male is a 'gom' or 'gommeril' and might 'have toys in the attic'. A 'yob' or a 'haverel' is an ignorant man.

'That fellow has the yellow kelters and plenty' – he is rich.

Horsy parlance spreads to affairs of the heart and bed in Kildare: 'She's good for a canter'; 'She's good over the hurdles'; 'She's a quare one on the back-stretch'. A diminutive jockey was 'knocking around' with a rather large lady, and the remark was passed that, if it came to anything, he would be 'like a pimple on the Hill of Allen'. I could be 'beat into a cocked hat' for that remark, or for quoting the rhyme:

> *The town of Naas is an awful place,*
> *Kilcock is just as bad,*
> *But of all the places I ever met,*
> *Well hump you, Kinnegad!*

'All to one side like the town of Newbridge.'

In Kildare they 'talk the hind leg off an ass', or can be 'as thick as a *double* ditch'. A hot tip that does badly is 'still running'.

'That's a hash one'; 'That's a horrid dirty day' – but be careful of that word 'horrid', for you might be 'thought the world of' and be called 'horrid good'. In either event, you are well liked.

A bad football forward 'wouldn't hit the Hill of Allen if he were tied to it'. Kildare sayings make great use of their one and only hill.

'I didn't see you for a month of Sundays; you're a cure for sore eyes; why didn't you drop in sooner?' An expression of concern at a long absence would receive the reply, 'I kept putting it on the long finger'.

'He's growing down like a cow's tail' – said of a youth who is not growing very fast.

'Greasing the pig's ear' is putting more wealth in the way of somebody already well feathered. If such a fellow was called upon to do something that he had hired hands for, he would say, 'Have I to keep a dog and do my own barking?'

'That fellow has something up his sleeve' – he is planning something.

'You'd think butter wouldn't melt in his mouth' – he looks innocent, but isn't.

'You're nothing but a rogue like the generations before you.'

'He'll ate us out of house and home.'

An old saying that originated when informers were in danger of meeting with an accident is now used in the case of persons who endanger themselves by talking too much: 'Don't open your grave with your mouth.'

'Isn't he the limit?' is said of a wild character. 'As busy as a bee'; 'an old fogie' (elderly person); a '*sí gaoithe*' (fairy blast – sudden wind), a 'gluggar' (rotten egg) – these are old expressions still in use. 'He was like a cat on a hot griddle' – a griddle was a flat iron disc for making bread, and the description for a fidgety person is excellent.

An old Kildare proposal would go: 'Would you like to be buried with my people?' If the proposal were accepted and 'childer' followed, the mother would have them all around her 'like Mother Carey's chickens' – even if she was 'as weak as a kitten' from 'caring for them morning, noon and night'. One of them might get 'as sick as a dog'. An older one might be 'on the *seachrán*' or out of work. But if his pals looked for money from him they were 'barking up the wrong tree' for 'you can't get blood from a turnip'.

The Curragh plains are cold, and on a winter's morning, 'it would freeze the arse off an eskimo'.

Laois and Offaly are paired in many respects and no less in dialect. They have done well. They have 'the divil's own luck', in fact, and their own addition to this saying goes: 'The divil's own children have the divil's own luck. No wonder there's hell to play around the Slieve Blooms!'

Don't judge a man from this area by his appearance for you can't judge a book by its cover. Keep your eye on his friends though, as you can say to him, 'Show me your company and I'll tell you what you are'. But if he surprises you by being with a decent girl, you might be the one to remark, 'He's not in the same street as her'. If he called to her house too often, he might 'wear out his welcome'. But as he's an ardent man and walking on air over the whole thing, if she scorned him itself, 'it's a long lane that has no turning'.

When he would eventually 'take the bull by the horns' and would come out with it to a girl, she might tell him to be off with himself, adding that he was 'reared on the hind teat of a *gráinneog* (hedgehog)'.

'Talk is cheap,' they say down around Erril in Laois, where they also say, 'It would be easier to move the Hill of

Knockahan'. If you 'bought a Laois or Offaly man for a fool', you'd be 'a long time out of your money'.

A Tullamore woman was quoted a ridiculous price for eggs. 'You can keep them,' she said, 'I'd be as well laying them myself, so I would!'

Don't believe a word of it if anybody tells you that an Offaly man 'wouldn't give a glass of water to his mother if she was dying'. And don't on your life repeat a word of it to him or he might 'cut the socks off you' or at least 'trim you down to size' some way or other.

'You have no call to carry on like that,' says a father who is reprimanding his daughter. 'Oh, how bad you are,' the daughter might well answer, 'and not a word do you ever say to to that bucko of a brother of mine. He's as lazy as sin, sleeps like a log till the day is well aired. When he does get out of it (the bed), he doesn't do a hand's turn from morning till night. I have the two hands worn off me from waiting on the two of you morning, noon and night, so if I have an odd fling, Father dear, you'll have to take the good with the bad, and the large spud with the *póirín* (small potato), and put up with me.'

'Begor, but that's woeful steam you have out of you, girl, but don't worry, I'll get shut of him (get rid of him) as sure as there's a bill on a crow,' says the father, softening toward his daughter for whom he has a great *grá* or soft spot at the back of it all.

'Well it takes all sorts to make a world,' says the daughter. 'A few minutes ago you were rantin' and ravin' at me – as cross as a bag of cats – and now, at the drop of a hat, you're all pie.'

'Ah, sure it's over and done with now so hold your tongue, daughter. Eaten bread is soon forgotten, girleen.'

'Well, I'll be damned,' says her ladyship – but she knew from the start that she'd be 'away in a hack' once she referred to the lazy lump of a brother.

A Westmeath woman who was widowed twice was said to

have 'put two men under in her day'. The same woman got little education. Indeed, she 'didn't know B from a bull's foot'. She got a man to do up the house on the strength of the second husband's will, and she only paid him £5 and 'the run of his teeth' (or 'his keep' – she fed him).

Well, 'it didn't matter a hat of roasted snow' to the workman for he was drawing the dole anyhow and was only doing the job as a 'nixer' (to earn extra money).

There was 'hell to pay', ructions, *rírá* and *ruaille buaille* on the day when the workman knocked down the wall-wagger ('wag-o'-the-wall' – clock with long pendulum) and made 'smithereens' of it as he was foostering around (fiddling – moving awkwardly).

'You're all eyes and no sight,' screamed the widow, and she gave the workman 'who began it' or 'the length of her tongue' (a severe reprimand).

'Mullarkey' (refers to any man) was a bit of a 'daltheen' (impertinent fellow), however, and he told your woman that the clock was 'out of the ark' (old), and that if she didn't stop 'catherwauling' (complaining) like a cranky (bad-tempered) old hen, he would walk out and she could 'go and jump in the lake' for herself and get somebody else to finish the job. Well, that brought the widow 'down off her high horse' (made her humble), so she 'let the hare sit' (said nothing more about the affair), and before the evening was out the couple were 'as thick as thieves' (were 'very great', 'all palsie walsie' – good friends again).

When Westmeath men and women' jump the bezum' (twig or broom), they marry. A mean-looking man is 'like something that fell off a tinker's cart and wasn't missed, and if you saw the divil running down the street with him crossways in his mouth you wouldn't say, "Drop him"'.

It is said of an unlucky woman: 'If it was rainin' soup, she'd have a fork', or, 'she's ate across'. To an unwelcome guest, you would say, 'Don't go without pulling the door after you!'

'He shnailed out of a side-road.'

'He has as much land as there's feathers on a frog.'

'He's as black as the Earl of Hell's riding boot' – this saying is common in Louth and Meath too and is often altered to '... the Earl of Kells' waistcoat'.

'Oh, they're well matched' – they're two of a kind.

'I'll be there, dead or alive or on horseback.'

Ballinalee is the birthplace of people poles apart – Seán MacEoin, the 'Blacksmith of Ballinalee', prominent in Ireland's fight for freedom, and Sir Henry Wilson, Chief of the General Staff of the British Empire who was assassinated during the same struggle. Ballinalee people change 'wouldn't know B from a bull's foot' to 'wouldn't know A from the gable end of a house'.

They don't get 'guggured', 'shagged', 'bet out' (beaten or spent) as they explain that the 'guggurrer' was the man that put the potatoes in the hole made by the 'skeeven', a device with a 'preb' on it (a 'lug' or wing) for making holes in the earth for sowing.

They tell of people 'with sharp points to their tongues' who are 'dyed-in-the-wool Fine Gaelers, who are crawlin' alive with fleas'. Then they tell a story prefaced by the explanation that 'a white shirt shows flea marks'.

They tell of the Sinn Féin courts that appointed their own magistrates to carry out justice and of some man being up for something in front of a magistrate of whom he said, 'I'm not coddin' you but he had a shirt on him like a fiddlers's notebook' – it had dots and crotchets, breves and semi-breves from flea marks.

Of a noisy woman, they say, as elsewhere, 'She was like a haggard of sparrows', but where the county joins Leitrim, or beyond, they say: 'She's like a corncrake. When you think she's finished she begins again.' Then a discussion starts on the corncrake and his abilities as a ventriloquist ... which leads to talk of the land.

'The spuds were so small he was throwing them into a five-naggin bottle.'

A man's prowess at turf-cutting was highly thought of in the country before the giant machine invaded bogs. Of a poor 'sleansman', it was said: 'He wouldn't cut as much turf as would make smoke for Benediction.'

'He'd talk to a brass band.'

'A good girl is hard to come by.'

'He wouldn't say "boo" to a goose.'

'They won all before them.'

'He gave me the space of a couple of drills' – he allowed me to grow two rows in his field.

Start an argument in Longford and 'one word will borrow another until it will come to blows, most likely'. 'He was dragged up', 'He was only half saved', they say of a contemptible fellow. If a Longfordman does not mind one way or the other, he says, 'I'm aisy', and if a lad is good at the sums, he's 'figuresome'. They still use the old anti-fairy talk when they throw out water in parts of Longford – *'Ruaille buaille*, Rigadoo, Huga-huga, *uisce sala'*. When mumps are present in a family, the water is thrown out with the remark, *'A mhuc, a mhuc, seo dhuit a' leicní'*, and I heard this incantation quite recently in Longford.

Posh people are 'Blue Bloods'. If it is snowing they say, 'They're plucking geese in Galway'. A roll of butter is a *'mioscán'* or a 'print'.

A Longford woman was telling her son about her father's death. She gave all the details of his death-agony, and finished her account by saying, '... and the last words he said were, "Bury me dacent"'.

'Did you catch anything?' asked of a fisherman might evoke the reply, 'Sorra a haypurt' (not a ha'penny worth). It was in Abbeyshrule that I first heard the saying, 'How's she cutting?' replacing 'How's it going?' – both meaning 'How are things with you?'

'While the sun shines and the wind blows, the world will still be going.'

'They never did a tap' – they were idle.

'They wouldn't hear tell of it' – they wouldn't heed.

'There's no guard on that one's tongue' – she'd say anything.

'The road turned and I didn't,' says a fellow that had an accident. He might also say: 'I ran out of road.'

'An angel's born!' – ejaculation used in thanksgiving, like 'Thanks be to God!'

'The language wasn't too Parliamentary' – it was 'choice' – bad.

'That one would pee paraffin oil' – she's a vicious woman.

A cutting description of a horse show was given by a Longfordman: 'A lot of horses showing their asses to a lot of horses' asses showing their horses.'

Dublin

Dear old dirty Dublin, the lovable city by the Liffey with its buildings full of character, its parks that are havens of rest in a bustling world of commerce, its meandering canals lined by trees, 'more sinned against than sinning', and, of course, its people: Dicey Riley, Biddy Mulligan and Lizzy Leonard – characters from street ballads drawn as prototypes from Monto, the Liberties or Summerhill. 'Jackeens' with an accent that defies imitation. The 'Dalymount Roar' and the shouts from the 'Dubs' on the 'Hill' drown the gems of wit and repartee that thrive among the people there. Seán O'Casey, Brendan Behan, James Joyce – world-famous figures weaned on the rich metropolitan tongue that at once can lash, cajole and entertain. Who else could describe a mean person so wittily? –

'He would peel an orange in his pocket', or, 'He turns down the gas when he wants to turn over the rasher', or 'He'd give you a fag once a week but that was yesterday'.

'He was gone out – like the mailboat.'

'He was no mean performer on the old gargle trap.'

'He's only a mouth' – a big-talker. 'He's the only man in the world who has to get Holy Communion on a shovel.'

'I'll be dug out of you' – I'll beat you.

'I'll beat you good-lookin'.'

'Your blood is worth bottlin'.'

'He'd drink porter out of a policeman's boot.'

'You're that sharp, you're in danger of cuttin' yourself.'

'You have the common gall to laugh into my face and I droppin' down dead of the dreuth for the want of a gargle' – the speaker is in need of a drink!

A 'steamer' or a 'spoofer' is one who talks too much about things he knows little about. A 'nibbie' is one who has some menial task like collecting dirty crockery in a catering establishment.

♟ ♟ ♟ ♟

A 'gouger', 'gurrier', 'cowboy' or 'gink' is a bad type of fellow.

'Don't squeeze me until I'm yours' means 'Don't take me for granted'. A 'mixum-gatherum' is a conglomeration of articles. A fellow who talks a great deal of nonsense but does little, merits the remark: 'If crap was music, that fellow would be a brass band.'

Brendan Behan perpetuated some glorious Dublin sayings and stories in a book that had as its title one such saying: *Hold your hour and have another*. When persons could drink late in a pub provided they lived more than three miles from it, they were know as 'bona fide travellers'. Maria Concepta, talking on and on in a pub, was halted with the words: 'You're rambling that far, you'll be bona fide in a minute.'

Persons coming to Dublin from the provinces are called 'culchies' (as rural folk coming into provincial towns are called 'mulchies' in places). Talk about 'the kettle calling the pot black'! Dubliners have accused their provincial brethren of coming up 'with the mark of the stirabout (porridge) spoon still on their mouths'.

A 'quare class' of a fellow could have 'a screw loose' or 'might not be playing with the full deck'. A cute person 'would sleep in your ear and let the other in flats'. A cold day is said to freeze certain reproductive organs 'off a brass monkey'.

A cigarette is a 'gasper', or a 'drag' on one would do a fellow a world of good.

'Have a dekko at that; run your lamps over it' – Dubliners having a look.

The 'ball and chain' or the 'trouble and strife' or the 'auld flower' is the wife. 'If she kept woolagoning about her splittin' headache, she would drive a fellow into the loony bin (the mental hospital).'

'Janey mac, that wouldn't make a dog hit his father. Will I hit him a belt in the kisser, Jem? Here, hold me coat and let me have him.' The demand to hold the coat was often a ploy for time, a concealed invitation to a third party to prevent the fight from taking place.

'A bullock is the splittin' image of a cow but it still doesn't give milk.' This refers to something that is not what it appears to be. 'Every mother's daughter of them is off to the Coombe every year to have their fourth or fifth jug of water' – the Coombe is one of Dublin's maternity hospitals and all the aforesaid is a comment on large families.

'He made a haymes of it'; 'He made a bags of it'; 'He ballsed it up' – putting it mildly, he didn't acquit himself too well! But if singing is being discussed, he did well if he 'raised the rafters' or 'brought down the house'.

'Carry on with the coffin, the corpse can walk' – an apt expression if irrelevant detail is being discussed.

'That fellow has no cop-on' – he is tactless.

'He kicked the traces' – he objected.

'He'll get his comeuppance', or 'He'll get what's coming to him' – both mean that he will get the treatment he deserves.

'That fellow swallied instead of chewed to save his delft' – he did not wish to wear out his false teeth.

A few 'scoops' or 'rosiners', 'balls of malt' or 'jorums' are drinks. If a fellow 'got it hard to bend his elbow', he was slow to buy, but if 'his elbow was up and down like a whore's drawers' or like a fiddler's, he was pulling his weight in the company.

A 'one and one' is fish and chips, which might give a fellow 'the backdoor trot' if 'it didn't agree with him'.

An 'e' is placed before 'z' in Dublinese: 'He'd ate a baby's bottom through the monkey's cage in the eZoo'. 'He scored a big ezero'.

Around the Pepper Canister church there stroll ladies who might be described as 'good things' or 'bicycles'. The whole 'caboosh' of them have 'plates of mate' on them as big as cops – they all have big feet. And to an innocent lad, they might remark: 'You little sparrow-fart. I'd suck you in and blow you out in bubbles.'

A Dublin 'chisseler' (child) does its 'ekker' (homework). 'I never enjoyed meself as much without laughin' as the day Anastasia told her auld bag of an aunt that the wart on her beak was like the Hell Fire Club on the Scalp. Oh it was brutal, so it was.'

'Deffiney' is the Dubliners' pronunciation of 'definitely'.

'Iddena?' means 'isn't it?' 'Despra' is 'desperate'.

'You're like the poless (police) – never where you're wanten.'

'Shockin'', 'Diabolical', 'Jaysus awful', 'Gapin'' – descriptive words for catastrophes.

'The sneaky lug took anythin' that wasn't nailed down and off with it under his oxter, a mile a minute.

'A hatchet-faced auld strap struck out her spague and down he come on his kisser. Well, he was like somethin' the cat drag-ged in, and what did he do only start to bawl?' – a description of the fate of a thief.

Royal and Wee Counties

North-east Leinster comprises Meath with its site of our ancient royal seat, Tara, and the lush and historic Boyne Valley, and Louth, the smallest county in Ireland, boasting some of our best prehistoric archaeological sites. Mining has brought a new vitality to the area, and progress has taken its toll of things traditional. The speech of the people of this area reveals a dramatically sudden change from the broad accent of of the Meathman to the near-Ulster tone of the folk around Dundalk.

'I'll hit you between the eye and the eyesight and you'll think the devil sent for you.'

'If he had as much larnin' as he has ignorance, he'd nearly be a schoolmaster.'

'Our fellow' is the brother, and 'our lassie' is the sister. Here 'runners' are 'blow-ins', and a retired man is 'out on grass'.

'She's a right gobaloon', they say of an '*óinseach*', a foolish girl. A similar man is an '*amadán*' and is 'only a ha'penny short of a shillin''.

'He's puffin' and spittin' like the Navan band.'

Giving directions in Ireland is an involved business and in the network of narrow roads off the fine main roads of Meath and Louth, it can be hazardous.

'You can't miss it' is a favourite saying – even when directions are given something like this: 'Whomsoever told you to come this way was a right lug. Turn about and you'll meet a

big crossroads with a *sceach* (bush) on it but don't mind it.
Keep on straight till you meet a "V" going right but you go left
and take the second corner past the green door. Go on past it
till you reach a right-hand turn but don't take it. Go up the big
hill at Connors' and go about a mile after that and you're
landed.'

'He has an eye like a travelling rat' means that he's quick
to size up or assess someone. Somebody that's new at a business or occupation is 'only a suckin' turkey'. While God is a
commissionaire in many counties, he appears to work overtime in Louth, for they say, in a troubled situation: 'God never
closes one door but he opens three or four others.'

'I'll never do it as long as there's a nib on a crow.'

Along the Louth-Monaghan border the expressions are
most unusual. A 'hausel' is the aperture for an axe-handle. A
'gulpin' is a rough man. A 'gazebo' is a big awkward man,
and a 'girsha' is a girl.

A simple fellow is described: 'The calf's slue is still on
him.' This, I am informed, has to do with the nodding head
and unsure gait of a new-born calf, but call me a 'whey-faced
get' if I'm wrong!

If a person is in a bad mess nowadays, he is said to be up a
certain creek that abounds in an unpleasant substance. North
Meath, Louth and Monaghan people, being more polite, prefer
to say: 'He's in fiddler's green and that's ten miles below Hell.'

I'll say, 'You're my old Sagosha' to my good friend, but if I
meet him up around Tallanstown, I might change it to, 'You're
a hook and sniffy for a garden gate'.

I 'swear to it on a stack of bibles' that a fellow who
thought I was taking his words lightly reprimanded me with
the words: 'You think I'm not an eejit at all!'

A widow left with a large number of children is 'left with
a heavy handful'. Her 'lazy bed' is not the result of her wid-
owhood, but a method of planting potatoes. A 'gilloroo' is a
fish, and a 'brough' is a halo around the moon that appears if
rain is imminent. 'Knots', 'wheat ears' and 'yellow legs' are
species of birds.

Next-door neighbours in a terrace of houses live under the roof with others and if they quarrel a bit they are 'not too great'.

'Bad scran to you' is a gentle curse. It appears to be connected with the similar ill-wish, 'May the roof fall in on you' – 'scran' in some places meaning thatch (but, more often, left-over food).

'Do you know what I'm going to tell you? Tom has a slate off?'

'Indeed and he has, and a ridge tile off as well.'

My parting saying from Louth and Meath and Leinster is undoubtedly of recent origin. It refers to a scantily-dressed girl, and it goes: 'She hasn't as much on her as would keep flies off a sugar bowl!'

Descriptions

I WOULD need to lay hands on the woman that would 'talk the hind legs off an ass' or 'the cross off an ass' back' to do justice to a section dealing with descriptive sayings. Some of these words and phrases are dealt with in their respective areas so we will concentrate on those that are used throughout Ireland. Unless they are extremely vague, explanations will be omitted – and even if that woman 'would talk to a haggard of sparrows' in some counties, let us ignore localities and get on with 'the father and mother of a job'.

'She's a street-angel and a house-devil.'

'He'd skin a flea for a halfpenny.'

'He wouldn't give you the steam of his pee.'

'The little runt was like a mouse in an elephant's ear.'

'He's as wild as a mountain goat.'

'He's as mad as a hatter.'

'He's as thick as a ditch.'

'He's as black as the Ace of Spades' (or a sloe).

A

♠

A

'He's as slow as a wet week.'

'If he turned sideways you'd miss him'; 'If he turned sideways and stuck out his tongue he'd be like a zip-fastener'; 'He's like a herrin' in a zip-fastener' (he's thin).

'She wasn't around when the good looks were being handed out' might not be quite as insulting as, 'She caught her face in the door', or, 'She was an awful lookin' streal'. 'Streal' often referred to dress rather than looks. 'She had a face on her that would stop a clock'; 'She had an arse on her like the back of a bus'. A diminutive chap dancing with such a lady and falling over her would be 'like a tender struggling with the Queen Mary'.

'She had hair on her like rats' tails.'

'She hadn't a pick on her' – she was very thin.

'She was as wild as a March hare.'

'She'd make you die laughing.'

'She was in the family way'; 'She had a bun in the oven'; 'She was up the pole'.

'She was moping around like a straying ass.'

'She was as dirty as a pig's crubeen.'

'That one is as old as the hills.' The women love to comment on another's age, and such a one sang at another's Confirmation party 'and she was no spring chicken even then.' 'As sure as there's a bill on a crow she must have been thirty if she was a day, but for the life of me I can't remember her exact age.'

'The poor little fellow wasn't tall enough to pick shamrock but he had a pair of eyes in him like bloodshot onions.'

'He wasn't too correct in the top storey' or 'The light was off in the upstairs window'.

'He had a smile on his face as broad as the Shannon.'

'He had a straight back on him as if he was after swallowing a crowbar.'

'He wouldn't let his left hand know what his right hand was doing.' 'He'd mind mice at a crossroads.'

'There wasn't as much sun as would put an undercoat on a bald head,' complained a returned holidaymaker. 'And the landladies are all robbers. There mustn't be as many landladies in heaven as would make a half-set. The place was full of Americans carrying on as if they owned the place. Little do they know that the Irish were walking to America before the flood. Some of them only went over there to see the time and they have accents you could sit up on. I'll tell you something for nothing, but, not a one of my ancestors could throw a stone but he'd raise a lump on a king's head. Quality, we were. Me father lay by the roadside one day and a big *bastún* of a landlord came by on his horse. "I say there, Sullivan," says he, "did you see the gentry pass by?" "I did," says me Da, "fifty years ago – and they never came back!"'

What dragged me onto that and I supposed to be giving descriptions? My stomach is 'falling out of me with the hunger' after it and 'I'd give my right hand (or my two eyes if I played the piano)' for a feed of boxty. But 'don't take me up till I fall, I'll carry on regardless'.

It is said of a fellow who acts as his father or mother did: 'It wasn't off the ground he scraped it', or 'His father will never be dead while he's alive'.

Stale bread is 'as hard as the hob of Hell'.

'You can take the man out of the bog but you can't take the bog out of the man.' And while I try again 'to cough up the turf-mould', let me tell you that I'm 'as stubborn as a mule', that I can 'sing like a lark' and that 'you'll be waiting till the cows come home' if you think that I 'give a tinker's dam' about 'any man Jack of you'.

Health and Worse – With Love

'WELL, AREN'T you the one that's lookin' half slack enough this while back! Now you're not given over for dead or anything but I wouldn't take a lease of your life.'

Irish people are not 'behind the door' when it comes to telling a person how bad they look.

'An Antrim man was found up to his oxters (armpits) in a bog hole. He had been stuck so overnight and was a sight when a search party came across him. He appeared to be suffering from exposure and everybody thought he was gone for the milk, that another clean shirt would do him, that he would kick the bucket.

'He was brought to the hospital where a big lump of a nurse with a pair on her like the buffers on the half-four from Sligo laid into doing something about him. This one had an eye on her that would see around corners, and didn't she spot that your man was as hoarse as a cuckoo when he tried to speak? Eyes are not often used for such diagnoses, but you have the hang of what I'm getting at.

'She immediately suspected that the patient was swingin' the lead, was draggin' his feet, that he fell over a straw and a hen picked him; in other words, that there was sweet shag-all wrong with him.

'She was as cross as a bag of cats when she asked him how long he was in the bog hole. "All night," says your man. When she asked him how he fell in the first place, he said it was the bog hole he fell in! He didn't open his mouth after that because she told him – chancing her arm – that she knew that he fell in the hole when he lost his way returning from a night on the ran-tan. She was right. She had hit the nail on the head.

'She could see that he was as hardy as a snipe, that he wouldn't tear in the plucking (had stamina), and that he'd be better before he was twice married and once a widower.

'"I'll go and get the surgeon to rip you open," she said, walking out the door, like a shot from a gun.

'Well that put the skids under his nibs. Out with him from blanket street and wasn't he gone like a cut cat through the window for there was nothin' on him that a good coort and a jar wouldn't cure.'

'It's lucky it's myself has the rheumatism. Himself has no thole' – he has a low pain endurance.

'He was wastin' away – his —— was no bigger than black thread! If I'm talking through my arse, I could always stitch it!'

'He's lookin' poorly. Sure he's a weeshy, wizendy wart of a weasel – alliteration is Wollickingly wonderful!'

'He's as sound as a bell.'

'He was better while you'd be saying " Jack Robinson".'

'He's as hardy as a mountain goat.'

'He's not looking any great shakes.'

'You'll get your death out in that weather.'

'How's the form?' 'Ah, poorly; I'm only pulling the Devil by the tail. If I was a building, I'd be condemned.'

'You could blow the poor divil off your hand, there was that little of him in it.'

'He's crawling with fleas. He's so dirty that if you flung him at the wall he'd stick.'

'He's gone to the dentist to get his delft subtracted.'

'That's an awful dunt he got. How is he?' 'Oh, he's stretch-ed; not a stir out of him – like a lump of bog deal.'

'How are you keeping, Tom?' 'Musha, Shakespeare is dead and I'm not feeling too well myself.'

It's amazing how many Irishmen die suddenly who have it said of them, 'He was never a day sick in his life'. There is a distinct reluctance to mention cancer by name. A knowing lift of the eyebrow, a 'wisha', or a very daring, 'Ah, he has the quare thing', is enough to convey that someone has the dreaded disease.

'I'm afraid he won't do any good.' 'His goose is nearly cooked.' 'He's going fast.' 'God help him, the last words he said *after he was gone* were, "Look after the children, Mary."'

About mentally retarded people, the Irish say, 'He's a bit soft in the head', 'He's a few bricks short of the full load', 'He's not the full shillin'', or 'He's not all there'. The Irish language references to such people are kinder.

'He's only a *leath-dhuine* (half person), God help him.'

'He's an unfortunate *leath-ceann* (half head).'

However, the most charitable and the loveliest way of expressing such a deficiency in a person is, thankfully, the one most widely used. It is 'He's a *duine le Dia*', the English form of which goes: 'He's one of God's children.'

When a person is dead and something is done which would have offended him, the remark is made: 'He'd turn in his grave if he knew that.'

'How are you today?' 'Oh nicely, thanks. Couldn't be better. No use complaining. You'll get nothing for it.'

'Divil a thing. Would you ever think poor Mick's Month's Mind was this morning?' – Month's Mind is a Mass said a month after death.

'You don't say! We won't feel it till he's being read out' – Being 'read out' means on the Altar List of the Dead, which is read out from the altar once a year.

If somebody is very fond of a place, they say, 'I'll never leave it till they take me out in a box' (a coffin).

Irish legends of sickness and death abound. Cuchulainn and Ferdia joined in battle by day and dressed each others' wounds by night.

Lough Gill is formed, it is said, from the tears of the nursemaid of the beautiful Gille who drowned herself when her father, Romra, slew her lover Omra, and then died himself from wounds received in the encounter.

'He's blind in one eye and can't see with the other.'

'He'd walk across a field and never see a daisy.'

🐧🐧🐧🐧🐧🐧🐧 🚶 🐧🐧🐧🐧

'He wouldn't see it if it jumped up and ate him.'

These sayings are as different as chalk and cheese from the lovely language of Ireland's lore. Yet they have a quaintness and a wit that makes them worth noting. Exclamations of admiration can often be gems:

'If you saw the chest and shoulders on his sheepdog, you'd be proud to be his father.'

'I can't retire. I have too many fine nephews and nieces to remember by and by.'

'The Big Wind wouldn't stir him' – The Big Wind of 1839 blew houses away.

'He's as lithe as a luarach' – a luarach is a long lath used in making a currach.

Obesity is often a problem with Irish people. Perhaps their love of eating well stems from the hunger endured during the famine. They disregard the advice: 'The best way to eat plenty of food is to eat a little good food so that you'll live long enough to eat plenty.'

'She always had a good roughness of food in the house.'

'She has a heavy table.'

'He has a great stroke,'

'He put back a huge feed.'

'He ate like a horse.'

'He nearly did away with plate and all.'

Conversations on health can take a peculiar twist at times:

'If poor Jim had lived another day the mother would have been a month dead.'

'God love him. He was no bother only he tired easily when he slept before he went.'

'I'm destroyed with the pains myself.'

'Are you taking anything for them?'

'I am then – punch.'

'I know a better cure.'

'Well keep it to yourself, I don't want to hear about it. Save your breath to cool your porridge. The whiskey is the only cure.'

'I believe you when hundreds wouldn't.'

'What's that? Did you say something?'

'Are you *leath-cluas* (half-deaf) or what?'

'Are you *leath-súil* (half-blind)? You're after walking into the water.'

'I'll get my death.'

'Indeed you won't. You're the picture of health.'

'How could I be and I after planting (burying) my husband only a month ago. I'm under the doctor since he passed on.'

'What doctor?'

'Dr ——.'

'He's a bloody horse-doctor (derogatory – he's a vet). You'll be fit for the knackers if you stay under him' – a 'knacker' is a fellmonger. 'You should go to Dr ——, he's out on his own.'

'I went to him once with a sprain and he gave me down the banks for annoying him with something so small – an' my ankle was out like a balloon. But I gave him the two barrels back, I'm telling you (I gave him everything, I told him off from a height).'

'I suppose I'd be adding fuel to the fire (exacerbating things) if I told you he has a right leg of the priest's housekeeper (gets on well with her).'

'That one. Faith then, she'll leave him light. She'd take the pennies from a dead man's eyes (She'll spend all his money and what she's not given she'll take).'

'She's a soft poor slob.'

'She's poorly.'

'I was sitting in the middle of the dinner when the doctor called.'

'My head was splittin'', or 'I had a splittin' headache', or, 'My head was opening'.

'The flesh just walked off him lately.'

'He was old for his age.'

'The teeth on my top are all right but the ones on my bottom are hurting me something terrible.'

'He was a cure' is a complimentary remark, meaning that he was a great fellow.

'You buried your wife since I saw you last, Jim?' The rhetorical question is asked of one expected to display a 'dacent' amount of grief. The surprise reply comes – the typical Irish question in answer to a question:

'What else could I do with her? Didn't she die?'

An inter-related, clannish population of a rural area was described caustically by a stranger who had not been made welcome: 'That crowd! If you gave a physic (dose, in this context) to one of them it would work them all.'

To a person who is concerned unduly about worldly things, who dashes here, there and everywhere in a hurry – 'like a whore on overtime' – is given the good advice:

'Musha, will you cool down, easy on out of that. Don't you know you can't take it with you, there are no pockets in a shroud.'

> *A useless, useful instrument,*
> *Bought for money, cannot be lent.*
> *The man who owns it, 'tisn't his own*
> *And the person it's bought for,*
> *It carries him home.* [A coffin]

'When Queen Elizabeth I was attempting yet again to bring the Irish chieftains to heel, the MacCarthy stronghold was at Blarney Castle, and she was having her fair share of trouble putting manners on their head buck-cat.

'Try as she would to get MacCarthy to reject his clan and

take tenure of his lands direct from the crown, he kept running with the hare and hunting with the hounds, to the extent that he had her in a complete hape (heap)' – she was flustered.

'He did not refuse the lady flatly, not wishing to offend her Majesty, he being behind her in the arms race. Neither did he accept her offer for he didn't want the rest of the Mac-Carthys breathing down his neck for the rest of his born days' – tormenting him for the rest of his life.

'He played for time with fair words and soft speech – as the lady described his *plámás*. One day, she sent yet another diplomat to parley with MacCarthy. This man returned with the same old rigmarole, the same old story, the same old tune – more "how's your father", more plámás.

'Although aeroplanes were unheard of then, the queen flew into a rage and screamed:

'"This is merely Blarney" – and that's how the use of the word originated. Oh, I swear it! God's truth!'

However, back to love, as the tennis player said when her partner lost his service.

'*Grá mo Croí* (graw mo cree)' – love of my heart! '*A grá*' is widely used to loved ones.

'They are getting on like a house on fire.'

'She's all pie when she's out, but a roaster (bad tempered) in the house.'

'That fellow's too sweet to be wholesome.'

'*Mo grá thú* (mo graw who)' – my love to you.

A greeting: 'Auld stock' – used in platonic friendships.

'She'll get her comeuppance.' This is said of a flirty girl who is 'divil-may-care', and treats her man lightly.

'She had a power of money and that's why he settled with her' – he married her for her money.

'There wasn't that much in her now would make a pickey' – she was as tiny as a small stone used in playing 'hopscotch'.

'I wouldn't put it past her to throw your man up. She might well let him down.' The contradictory terms both mean breaking it off or discontinuing walking out with a fellow.

'Kathleen Mavourneen' – Kathleen, my love. The song title is now used to describe 'the never-never' or hire-purchase system.

'Eileen Aroon' – *rún* is a secret or secret treasure. The air of the song is said to be the oldest harp air extant.

'Allanagh' – used more to children, *leanbh* being the word for child.

'She's a woman I can't warm to.'

'The kettle is on the boil there' – there's something between them; there's more than the eye can spot between them. 'They are getting great', or 'great with each other'. They are 'knocking around with each other'. They are 'doing a line', or courting.

'She rubbed him up the wrong way'; 'She nettled him'; 'She got on his nerves'; 'She drove him mad'; or 'She nearly drove him up the walls'. How inadequate is the clinical term, 'incompatible' beside these!

'She's no spring chicken: she's getting on a bit and because she's getting older she fears being left on the shelf or becoming a wall-flower (spinster).'

'She does nothing but stravigue around after every fellow.'

Advice given to a Kilkenny fellow who was afraid to 'pop the question': 'A dumb priest never got a parish.'

'Troghs and she wasn't that great a catch!'

'She's a right go-by-the-road.'

'She tied him up in knots and every time he opened his mouth, he put his foot in it.' This does not describe a contortionist's act in a circus. It means that she baffled him and he kept making blundering remarks.

Dublin cornerboys shout after the 'mots', 'hens' or 'birds'. The girls hit back that they are called birds because of the worms they pick up. They abuse 'flies':

'Me hand on your drawers.'

'Would you risk it for a biscuit?'

'Kiss me for a lark.'

'Come out to the Scalp and we'll have a rare auld time.'

'Where did you get all the raddle (lipstick)?'

They get on 'like Bohs and Shels' – like two rival soccer teams, Bohemians and Shelbourne.

'You've an arse on you like the Ballast Office.'

'And your own is no pimple.'

'All your pimples are on your face. It's like a bowl of pearl-barley soup.'

'Ah, shut your face.'

A girl might complain about someone in the lad's family who is spreading yarns about her. If a confidence is broken, she says, 'There's a hole in the house'.

However, they would get over their grievances and would soon be 'like Granny Gariosch's cat', all hugger mugger, and happy as the day is long.

'Ah, me aul' flower, my sweet contemptible!' – the contradiction is a compliment.

'Will you go away – you should still be boxin' the fox.' This is said by a girl to a fellow she considers too young for her. 'Boxin' the fox' was hanging out of travelling coal-trucks and knocking the coal lumps off.

'He's a dotey little fella' – he's lovely.

'That babby of theirs is like the butt end of a tumbler – always wet.'

'What would we do at all without the menkinds?'

Expressions of love in Ireland are not of the Romeo and Juliet quality. Men still demur when it comes to expressing their love in public. It is considered almost unmanly. But the girls accept this and they don't make 'Blind Billy's bargain'.

This has nothing at all to do with love, but is used in finishing the section to demonstrate the fickleness of man.

The Limerick hangman was called 'Blind Billy'. Because of his disability and his occupation he had to have an escort at all times. Well, one day he refused to execute a hanging until he was paid £50 in cash. After much arguing, the £50 was paid by the city fathers, but after the job was done, they refused to provide Billy with an escort until they got the money back.

Poor Billy! You get no thanks for anything. They should be strung up! Not one of them would have your job for love or money.

Ulster

On Lough Neagh's Shores

NORTH OF Portadown in the 'Orchard county' of Armagh there is an area known as the Montiaghs. In nearby Breagh, there lived in the nineteenth century a man named William Lutton. William departed this life on 2 November 1870 but left a legacy of assorted results of research into the ways of the countryside around Lough Gullion on Lough Neagh's shore. No mean musician, he built himself an organ, so it is not surprising that he had a passion for collecting the old words and phrases that flowed in melodic cascades from the lips of his country folk. 'If you whisht you'll hear the yellagh of the yowtlin' – if you are silent you'll hear the child's laugh. The child might well be laughing at his 'whigmaleeries' – his toys, or at another 'wean' – 'wean' is the common Ulster term for a child.

Letters were sometimes pasted on a type of board to teach children the alphabet, and this board was known as a 'batley board'. In the schoolroom, 'caddis' was placed in inkwells, and it was simply some substance that soaked the ink, thereby preventing it from spilling.

School playgrounds might boast a 'shuggey shoe' – a rope for swinging off, and a ride on a 'shilty' brought many a 'skit to a skilt' – a pony ride produced a bit of 'gas' for a lively girl.

White lies, fibs, harmless untruths are known as 'slents'.

They are part and parcel of many a 'shanagh'. The conversation known as 'shanagh' usually occurs after a homecoming.

'The sheela was sherpet after the shurl.' This is not a tongue-twister but a collection of words which convey that a sissy of a man who involved himself in the affairs of women was shaken after a fall. The same fellow might have been a 'cawdey' (a cute sort of chap) as a youth. The women with whom he became involved might have been 'cooney', 'cornaptious', 'denty', 'dyled', 'eye-bright', 'loopy' or 'sloamy' – they could be cautious, irritable, tidily dressed, stupid, handsome, sly or plain lazy.

Droll sarcasm can be a feature of the Armagh people.

'Lord, but I'm glad to rest. I'm set up (tired). I only walked from the Post Office and my feet are killing me.' This expression of fatigue, far from receiving a sympathetic word, might merit the retort:

'That's what comes from being reared in your bare feet.'

A boy was heading home after school in a Down village. He was accompanied by his older brother who was asked by a passer-by why the younger lad was covered with mud. The older brother explained:

'He took a ram stam at the slithery slurry and come a right sprackle in the sheugh. His ma'll warm him proper' – the lad fell in the slippery mud, and his mother was going to beat him (to lambaste him might be a more appropriate term).

A boarding house sign in County Down reads: 'Young men taken and cared for'. Caring for them might have prompted the Down landlady to remark to her new lodger that he had 'a heavy stroke' – a good appetite. 'Aye,' said the lad, 'me mother often said I was handy at the trough.'

Remarks on landladies could be complimentary, but more often caustic: 'She's right full of herself'; 'She has a swelled head'; 'She thinks she's it'; 'She thinks there's none to touch her.'

'She would make trouble between two breast-bones.'

'She's a right clippin' of tin.'

The lady's cooking might be described as 'slysterin', and if it merited that adjective it would not receive any knife and fork awards. if she were described as a 'snapper', on the other hand, her cuisine was beyond reproach.

Should she use 'snash' to her lodgers, they might counter with a 'snig' – abuse receiving derisive repartee.

If an extra guest came to her table, he would have to take 'pot-luck'. This term, originally used with reference to joining in the family meal, is now universally used to describe any situation in which one must take what is available.

The *póirín* or small potato is called 'por-yey' in parts of Armagh. The clinging goose-grass that is stringy and sticky is called 'Robin-run-the-Hedge' here and in many other country areas. Coarse flax is 'rablogh', a cabbage stalk is a 'runt' (a small man is often given this derogatory title too), small apples are called 'scrunty', and there is a type of iris known as 'saggans'.

At an Antrim wake the widow of the deceased greeted an old friend and, after the usual sympathising, the guest was ushered into the wake-room where the widow produced the bottle of spirits, presented the sympathising friend with a glass, and remarked, 'He always had a smack for you, Mary. You'll drink his health now, won't you?'

When the two women returned to the 'parlour' to talk about other things, Mary remarked on how well the widow's front garden was looking.

The widow did not agree, saying that her husband's illness had left her with little time to tend the garden. 'To tell you the God-honest truth,' she said, 'I've never seen my front so far behind before.'

When the discussion turned to her child who had failed her examination, Mary remarked, 'The unfortunate wee thing never passed a thing after stewing her brains for days.'

'She's an awful lookin' gammerel'– a 'gammerel' is a piece of timber that is passed through a carcass for hanging. The description is mainly given to a tall, thin person. A 'boghal' is a bad craftsman. A 'beddy bel-yore' would be a meddlesome and talkative person. Not 'caring a rap' is a common expression, but in old Ulster parlance a 'rap' is a scoundrel.

A 'skree' of potatoes is a large number of them, and a 'slipe' is a type of cart without wheels used to drag potatoes or other items through marshy land. A 'bletherumskite' or 'skite', is a nitwit or frivolous person. A 'neyerk' is a constant complainer who is ever 'whingeing' (crying) over things.

Sometimes a man would feign interest in a girl because she or her people kept a good table. This fellow would be labelled a 'belly bachelor'. A man who married a Belfast lady who was noted for 'scrimping' or cutting down on the food had this said of him: 'All their hens are pensioners for he married a city one and she'd kill off nothin'.'

A woman, commenting on her shrewd buying, was once heard to remark: 'I wouldn't buy a rabbit without its head for fear 'twould be a cat.' And speaking of buying, the bell whose clapper is struck as a customer enters a shop is considered old-fashioned, but what about the Armagh shop that has a jamjar with a spoon inside on the counter, and the notice: 'Rattle For Attention'? What a descriptive saying for a fussy person is 'auld flutter-guts'! And could a sickly person be better observed upon than with the remark, 'She's as white as a clout (cloud)'? A sour-faced man earned the remark: 'Sowl, if he died with that face nobody would wash him.' His bad-temper might evoke the expression: 'He has taken the rust.'

A Carrickfergus man was 'bothered with the rheumy in the hinch bone', while his wife was 'harrished to death by the weans'. Nor could the doctor help her for she was 'awful bad at swallying pills'. Not fancying their son's unkempt appearance, they derided his 'hair like dulse (a seaweed)'. He was a 'skelly-eyed drouth with a mouth the size and shape of a pint tumbler'.

Men of the land pay little attention to details that might puzzle the visitor. Fruit is either ripe or 'green'. An American asked an Antrim farmer about ripening berries on the hedge:

'What are those berries?'
'Blackberries.'
'But those berries are red.'
'That's the colour they are when they're green.'

Something that's dreadful or odious is 'oojus', and, if something is hideous altogether, it is 'hi-oojus'.

'He's neither well nor sick but he always bees girning' – complaining.

> *As round as a griddle,*
> *As flat as a pan;*
> *A half of a woman,*
> *The whole of a man.*

Those who remember not the currency that preceded decimalisation will not recognise the English penny in the above rhyme.

'He's wizened and won and he's wheezling' – shrivelled and dried up and is wheezing.

'That's a fair blirt in it' – that's a rainy wind.

'Give it a good dunner' – knock loudly on the door.

'Go and wash the glit off your hands' – 'glit' is mud.

'He hadn't a steevan in him for a week' – he hadn't a full meal for a week.

'Bring it back here, rap or run' – get it by fair means or foul.

'Bring a boon to the threshing' – bring a gang of workers.

'Wit' means 'sense' in Ulster as well as in most Irish country places. 'He hasn't a tittler of wit' means he has no sense, and an Antrim parent might exhort her child to 'hov a wee bit o' wut'.

'Whose owe is thot spade?' – who owns that spade?

'Give me it here I want to dig a trinket (drain).'

'The stroup is dreepin' – the spout is dripping.

'There's somethin' duckery-pawkery goin' on' – there is some intrigue taking place; something is not above board.

'I went to Larne yesterday on a petrol bus.'

'I wish the pain in my head would go. If I hadn't it all the time I'd think there was something wrong with me.'

In Ulster, the word 'authorise' is used in place of 'correct': 'He'll catch it from me for he needs authorising'; The farmer that was exercising a lively dog 'authorised' him so: 'Ach come away along back ower thot. Did I no tall you te come in ahine afour?'

A family was trying to persuade an octogenarian uncle that he would be better off in an old folks' home than trying to fend for himself. Having pointed out the merits of the place and having described it for the old man, a bachelor all his life, the reply they got was, 'I think I'd like it fine but they're right and dangerous places, all the same. I've nodged (ambled) along nicely up to this and avoided the weddin' bells and I'll not be pleasin' ony wee nursin' girl to get her picture on the papers now.'

Large lips must have some attraction in Antrim. Some people claim that members of a certain denomination are 'tight-lipped'. In any event, a girl might well be described thus: 'She's nice but she has a wee thin mouth on her.'

Of an injury to a man's leg there came the remark: 'It's only bleedin', better bleedin' nor beelin' (festering).'

To 'narl' is to 'nark' or complain.

A 'snaffle' is not some sweetmeat, but a bad type of character, one who might be 'nurled' (undersized) but who is a bit of an 'owlhan' (crafty, looking after himself) who would 'blast' (praise) you to your face, but would knife you at the same time. He would be one of the 'riff-raff' (low type) who would 'tossicate' (stir up trouble) and then 'vanquish' (disappear).

An Armagh woman was back home feeling somewhat fed up, having had atrocious weather on her hard-earned holiday at Portrush. 'We came away early for there was no sense in paying hard money for the view,' she remarked.

A clockin' hen has a mind for hatching her clutch (feels like hatching her eggs) – perhaps 'at the heel of the evening' (at twilight). She might have her eggs in an old 'kesh' (turf basket) or 'kimlin' (tub). A 'langel', 'spenchal' or 'spancel' might be tied on the hen's legs to prevent her from wandering. The kesh might be in the 'skey', a makeshift shed, or even near the comfortable 'logie', which is the firedoor of a kiln. But then, of course, the old hen might be a 'swaddy', all overweight – or 'stubbly', the opposite. In this event, she would be part of a 'rite-therie', a group of worthless domestic fowl.

'What were your spuds like last year?'

'They were wee.'

'How wee?'

'You could put two or three of them in your gob at the one time and talk to the neighbours.'

This type of conversation is far removed from the dialect words, many of Gaelic origin, set down by William Lutton. But Lough Neagh is surrounded by Down, Antrim and Tyrone as well as Armagh, and the humorous conversation recorded above could well have originated in any of these counties. Ulster anecdotes are difficult to set down on paper, for their real charm lies in their narration in the tongue of their people. How can you effectively write the lovely command of the marching bandleader who holds his staff aloft, draws himself up to his full height and bellows:

'Win, two! Flutes to the mooth! Quick march!'

Or the old man who was given his first cigar at his granddaughter's wedding and asked his son, holding the match to the long Havana: 'Dae ye see ony smook commin' frae me?'

Patsy Fagan, that 'harem-skarem, divil may carem daecent Irish boy' may have come from Neagh-side, for 'herim-skerrim' aptly describes a lad like Patsy. A 'haikey' is a silly person, a 'knawky hal-yan' is a crafty good-for-nothing, and a 'harl-o-bones' is a thin person (or animal). A 'how-dey' is not a country and western greeting, but a midwife who might urge her charge to 'hap' or wrap herself up in warm clothes. This good lady often had to 'pindther' or work for little remuneration. She was often regarded as a 'spae-woman' too. This title made her a type of fortune-teller.

'It will take you all your time to get anything out of him.'

'The Lord will open a gap for him' – God will find a way for him.

'Take a wee geek' – Have a wee peep.

'Have a skelly out the back' – Have a peep out the back door.

To wash clothes or other objects in water is to 'suddle', while dampening of dough is 'sappling'. This term is applied to all wetting of materials. A 'scawn' is a badly-baked cake, and a 'clart' is an unhygienic housekeeper. She might use a 'coppen for a poghal of slim-cake' – a wooden vessel for a small quantity of potato-cake.

In parts of Ulster, mainly in rural areas around Glengormley, Dundrod, Kilrea and again along the Holywood Hills, Dundonald, Carryduff and Boardmills, a Scotch accent is still distinguishable. A married man is described as a 'weeda-maun' while a 'bauchalor' might have 'haud a notion o merrien a lauk o times'.

If a Tyrone drinking companion had to be assisted home, it would be said that, 'Sam and me had tae oxtercog Jamie hame', although 'oxtercog' is also the acquisition of an article under dubious circumstances. 'Canavaun' is bog cotton in Tyrone as well as elsewhere, and a 'ferox' is a trout.

A poor Tyrone woman would have 'neither in her or on her', not even a 'snoot cloot' to wipe her nose. If she met a fellow townsman she might remark, 'Away to hell, are you from Cookstown?' If she lost her shoe, she would be 'havin' a wee geek for the neighbour of my shae'. Boys and girls here are 'cubs and cubbies', the 't' of west Ulster being softened to 'b'. This lady might speak in admiration of a man thus: 'A hardy fraction of a man that would have wrestled a monkey in a sack', and if the Tarzan happened to need a haircut, he might instruct the barber to 'stripe it off brave and close 'cause it's naught but a harbour for vermin'. A Tyrone snack is a 'gutser', a 'sup of tea' is a mugful, not an arbitrary amount as 'sup' implies elsewhere. Foodstuffs have been called 'comestibles', sweets called 'jubes', ends of ham called 'knobs', and if in need of these foodstuffs, a person would declare that his tummy was 'churnin''.

Indeed, the counties surrounding Lough Neagh have a wealth of peculiar expressions concerning food. 'Colcannon' is a well-known concoction of potatoes, parsley and onions, but 'praties and point' is an expression to describe a frugal meal. When potatoes were placed on the bare table, the younger members of a family merely pointed their potato at the butter which was reserved for the parents.

The cup of tea and the chat beloved of women is called a 'collogin cup'. This is based on the word 'collogue', meaning to talk confidentially. The guest who reached for the wedge of apple cake at the end of such a repast and remarked 'Thanks very much, this will finish me', hardly meant to insult her hostess. Had she called the piece proffered a 'scradyan', however, it would have been a different kettle of fish, for that meant a miserable, worthless piece.

Belfast

Even amid the strife-torn, polarised communities of Belfast city, old expressions survive alongside humorous sayings whose origins are in the troubles with which that metropolis is afflicted. The late Jimmy Young was a man who brought a ray of jocular hope to a tortured people of all denominations, and his anecdotes live on. Like the two old ladies on the bus who heard a man standing in the aisle say to his mate, 'We'll pinch those two old birds' seats when they get up'. They spoke of an accident that they had witnessed: 'The car kept going sidey-sidey till nothing would do it but take the wall wid it', and of an ailing acquaintance they remarked, 'Wee Hughie's away to scrapin's. I only saw his frame goin' along the road'.

The 'troubles' brought their share of unintentional witticisms too. 'They were all cloddin' but he fired the scraw at the harl o' bones' – he threw the sod at the thin person.

'Thon's a fly boy' – he is cute.

'Please, God, mind yourself for if anything happens to you we're all done for,' prayed a child.

'Patrick had to go to hospital with his head.'

The mother tried to console her child who asked: 'Is that a bawm?' with the reply: 'No daughter, just a hen layin' its wee egg.' Seeing men being taken away by the police, a woman remarked, 'They were all handcuffed by the feet'. Her advice to her son as she saw the police approaching her house was, 'Whatever you say, say nothing'. Of a neighbour in jail, she remarked, 'The gorb, he won't be long in for that fellow would ate his way through anything'. 'He got away last night' did not refer to an escape but to a death. Telling a child to rush for a doctor, she said, 'Hurry with your heels touching your head'.

Rubble is a plentiful commodity in Belfast. Commenting on a pile in her street, a lady said, 'You'd need to have a mighty striddle to climb over yon'.

Even the telling of a tragic event does not deter a Belfast woman from expounding with irrelevant detail, as in this account:

'The sun was splittin' the trees and I said to myself that I would walk a bit for the dog needed exercise. When I was bending around by Mrs Watson's, she was out trimmin' the bit of a wee hedge that she has about her house, and I bid her the time of day and got talkin' about whether her man was well or not. He was in hospital with a touch of the heart, God between us and all harm. I was just tellin' her how my Sam only lasted a few months after his cornery when who did I see coming down the street but Mrs Quirke. Just as I was goin' to give her the cure for the hives that she was askin' me about the Thursday – sprinklin' salt on the sheets and goin' to bed in the pelt – there was this unmerciful bang and a car blew up before my very eyes. The poor man in it was an awful sight. It sickened me so much I wasn't able to eat the bit of hoke-stey I had for the dinner.' ('Hoke-stey' is a rushed dish of bits and scraps.)

'Ah coudna be bothered with eatin' spare ribs for they're nathin' at all but a rickle o' bones.'

'Her an me's havin' a birl.'

'The hungry hoor is still catchin' up on the war rationing.'

'The last couch we had was a sofa.'

'I was after a feed of onions and put my feet up and there came a big bang you could hear for miles – the gas works blew up.'

Being finicky about food in parts of Belfast is being 'beddy'. As a reward for running an errand, a child might get a 'capper' which is a slice of bread with sugar atop. If a drinking partner is slow to order but eventually asks his mate to have a drink, he might reply: 'Thon's yin thing A'll no deny for you're this hour slabberin' like a boilin' pot.'

Belfast has its contradictions: 'Isn't he the brave coward?'; 'Come on away in. We're havin' a bit of a night out'. Asked the time, a Belfast person might reply: 'Five minutes and it would ha bin ten when I left home and our clock is ten minutes fast.' 'I know the trouble is bad but the television blows things up.'

As in many parts of Ireland, 'lettin' on' is pretending. 'Stickin' out a mile' is obvious but in Belfast 'sticking out' can also mean excellent. 'It's boggin'' means it's dirty; a 'shade' is a parting in the hair; and a 'tall' is a towel. While a 'wee dote' is a lovable child, a 'wee lump' is a fine child.

Think of the poor woman's discomfort who was 'waitin' on a pencil'!

Let us leave Belfast with my remark: 'As God's ma judge, A swear it nivver.'

Donegal

The Barnesmore gap funnels one into the wide wandering world of the Blue Stacks, Derryveagh, and on into the heart of Inishowen, swept by the Atlantic winds that find their way down narrow Lough Swilly, the Lake of Shadows, where 'a wee drop o' the scotch' finds its way into the dialect as well as into the glasses of the people. Bundoran, Ballyshannon and Donegal, south of 'Biddy's', as the Gap and its convenient hostelry are known, are cut off from the remainder of the county in accent and in expressions. You will hear the county's favourite and fulsome flower, the rhododendron, called 'Rhodydandrums', and they will tell you that their footballers will be 'hard put to it to win with the crowd of gastrals they have playing', 'gastral' being an uncomplimentary way of describing somebody. But one must pass through the Gap and wend one's way across the foothills of the Blue Stacks to pick up the true gems of Donegal's musically lilting colloquialisms.

A young boy is a 'caddy', and he escorts not a golfer, but a wee girl, known as a 'cutty'. 'Ah, cutty dear, how're you doin'?' you say to a girl, and you might describe the gender make-up of a family thus: 'They have three caddies and two cutties.'

'It be to him for he was puttin' the delft in the jawbox' – roughly translated: It must have been he because he was putting in his false teeth.' A 'flogger' is an overcoat; 'bawn' is a fort, and if you saw 'a pair of haverels in haults', you would be seeing two rather stupid fellows wrestling with each other. A 'gulpin' is also a 'haverel', particularly 'a thick gulpin'.

Should you notice a farmer trying to force an unwilling cow into a field, he would almost certainly be calling the animal an 'aul' trahn'. A 'trahn' is an 'unbiddable' animal – that is to say, it is stubborn about going where one bids it to go. The same type of animal might be described as being 'very brucklesome'. The Cavan expression 'cove' is also found in Donegal. 'Hello, cove' is a familiar greeting.

Sectarianism rears its ugly head in the expressions of the people, and a fellow threatening to 'lay into' a crowd (take them on in a fight), might threaten, 'I'll take them out of a face the way the devil takes the Protestants'. Incredulity is commonly expressed throughout the country with terms like, 'Ah, for God's sake!' 'Ah, who do you think you're coddin'?'; or 'Ah, you're havin' me on!' Donegal has a delightful way of expressing disbelief in what one has been told. It stems from the fact that the hamlet referred to once had but small, single-storey houses, and is said with a lift of the eyebrow and a sideways movement of the head: 'Ah, were you ever upstairs in Ballymagorry?'

The industrious people of Donegal have no time for a drone (the name comes from the lazy bee). They have their own name for him. It is 'osin', pronounced '*oshun*'.

'I'd stand black for him. I wouldn't let him down. I would stick to him through hell or high water.' And that's what I'd do for the great-hearted people around this lovely county.

But then why wouldn't they be warm and friendly? Wasn't the bed of Ireland's greatest lovers there? Diarmaid and Gráinne had their bed in Croaghlin, near Teelin.

Around Lough Erne

He'd drink Lough Erne dry' is a favourite saying about a hard man for the booze, a heavy drinker. It is a saying heard all over Ireland, and it is not used in introduction to decry the good people of Cavan, Fermanagh and Monaghan to whom we listen in in this chapter.

A Cavan man would have prefaced the aforesaid with the remark, 'I wasn't going to be cornabbled' (compromised). A story is told of a Cavanman who had a prize bull on loan from the Department of Agriculture. He did not return it within the stipulated period and an inspector of the Department duly arrived at the man's farm. To his horror, he saw the prize bull yoked to a plough, being roared at by the ploughman as it laboured through the rough soil: 'Get up, you bastard! I'll show you there's more to life than romance.'

'He's a caution'; 'He's a howl'; 'He's a sight' – terms for a devil-may-care type of lad who might be going around 'with both ends in the ground from making pancakes' if he were a Cavan bachelor. He might also have 'a tongue that would lick a calf' – and that would make him talkative. His marshy land might be called 'bottom', so if he had a fire going there, it might be said that there was 'smoke coming from his bottom'.

A woman who buys expensive things might merit the remark: 'She must have a gearcanai in the corner.' The same lady might kick up a row 'for the lucre of sixpence or so'.

A thin man 'must have been bet back from the trough', and if his nose is pointed, 'He had a nose that would pick a pot'. Despite his sex, a man would be called a whore – if, believe it or not – he was a likable fellow. This expression has grades and, depending on his popularity, the fellow can also be a great whore or a 'thunderin' great whore'.

'There'll be the devil to pay.'

'Up and down Cootehill riding Beelzebub.'

'It's a holy terror.'

Meet a Cavanman and you might say simply, 'Ocho!' Meet him again within minutes and it demands a more elaborate greeting: 'That's the way.'

Monaghan is known as the 'County of the Little Hills' and as 'Farney County'. One of its most illustrious sons was 'Parra Glas' or 'Green Paddy', a Rapparee who was 'not as green as he was cabbage looking' or who would be put off by a few 'cnocs'. We are told that Paddy lived in a cave near Tullgillen and that '*one* of his women had a hut in the Glen near Monaghan'.

Paddy would have 'skedaddled around' with his cronies, having fought with the defeated Jacobite forces, and, as we have seen, he was 'partial to the bit of skirt.' He may often have had 'his belly stuck to his back with the hunger' and what his girls complained about probably 'went in one ear and out the other'.

He was often tempted 'to tie the knot', but 'you can't teach an old dog new tricks', Paddy thought, until he did marry a peasant's daughter who admired his greenish-grey beard.

'You have me a great trake for nothing,' he may have said after walking miles to meet a 'targe' (or 'barge' – a nagging woman).

A mugful of 'strippings' of the milk – the last and best to come at milking – a plateful of 'stelk' (mashed potatoes and vegetable), and Paddy would be 'keeping a calm sough' (resting without talking) after his travelling.

Should Paddy have been inquiring of his woman's breeding, he might ask: 'What sort of broughtin' up did you get?' He would be told: 'Better than the brungin' up you got.' Having decided that the woman would 'give him a good run for his money', Paddy would start 'moping around her like a sick calf' or 'like a duck in thunder'. If he were gentle, the lady would take to it 'like a duck to water', but if he behaved 'like a bull in a china shop', she would 'give him his walking papers'.

If he placed his two hands together to scoop up meal or corn, he would have a 'gowpin'. He might fetch a 'go' of water from the well for one of his 'flipes', or he might say, 'I'll turn a ring on her nose' – a favourite expression of contempt.

Poor Paddy was 'trig and dacent (trim and neat) of a Sunday'. On other days he might have a half a foot of '*clábar*' (mud) on him. Some of his women might have been nearly 'past their market' or in a bit of a panic in case they might not get a man, with middle-age approaching. One might be 'sitting in the *gríosach* ' (red ashes), 'letting a trevallie (litany of curses) at him'.

'Gushers' or 'Trihens' were socks with no soles. A 'gorb' was a glutton, and a 'glunter' was a silly fellow.

A 'gleag' was a fistful of straw, and soft turf was known as 'fum'. A 'dull' was a loop in a piece of string – perhaps used to repair the 'creepy-stool' by the hob. A 'clarsha' was a slovenly woman, but a 'classy' was a drain running through a cowshed.

> Ballybay for makin' tae,
> Monaghan for brandy
> Carrickmacross for Pitch and Toss
> 'Blaney for cakes and sugar-a-candy.

A Ballybay woman sent her son for a message and he took a long time on the errand. Her remark to him was: 'You'd be the right one to send for trouble. You'd be a brave while bringin' it.' She did not like a photograph of herself: 'I don't take good from the front because I look better from the side only I'm thicker that way.'

Of a spinster, she asked what she would do if she found a man under her bed one night. The spinster replied: 'Under the bed? I'd tell him he'd be more comfortable under the blankets.'

Asked why she didn't ever marry a farmer, the spinster said: 'I'm not goin' to spend my days slutherin' around a farm.'

The woman's son got a chill because his boot was leaking. She told the spinster: 'Jimmy was absent from school because of his diarrhoea through a hole in his boot.'

'How is Mrs Gogarty?' 'Oh, she's mendin'. She got up yesterday and washed her face and hands on her feet.'

At the Summer Assizes, held on 24 April 1711, Patrick Glass O'Connolly was presented to be a 'robber, Tory and Rapparee, out upon his keeping, in arms and not amenable to the laws, but plundering His Majesty's good subjects'.

> *From Carrickmacross to Crossmaglen,*
> *There are more fathers than married men.*

And so to the county of the Erne proper. Fermanagh is completely divided by Upper and Lower Lough Erne, and right at the meeting spot, in the centre of the county is its fine county town of Enniskillen.

'Did you see e'er a word of a black-avised fellow comin' the way you travelled?' If you did see a sign of the black-looking fellow, it would hardly be a good Fermanagh man.

'How is every rope's length of you?' might be the greeting in Ballinmallard or Kilsherry, and you might be given a 'wheen' of apples from a woman of the house with a 'cuideog' (wrap) thrown over her shoulders.

'I got a right gunk' means 'I got taken in' (was cheated). A 'golder' is a scream, and a clutch of chickens is a 'clatch' here.

Spilling in from Tyrone are the sayings 'My thank-you bag is full' – I'm under a compliment; and 'They were reared on soot' – they were extremely poor. Americans may not like to know that a north Fermanagh man described a nasal American accent thus: 'His chat came down his nose.'

A wife who became fed up of her man under her feet all day would tell him he was 'always clockin' in the ashes'. Outside is 'outby', sneering is 'carring', and if a man keeps a 'moilie', he has a cow with no horns from birth. What a lovely way of describing well-cooked porridge is the following:

'I don't like it when it says "clip-clap". I only likes it when it says, "puff, puff, puff".'

A description of an old man's walk goes: 'He has a speng in his loins and is walking with a wee bit of a halt.'

Arriving at a doctor's door, a man told the receptionist, 'I have a wild achin' foot and I wondered if the doctor could make a hand of it!' That Cavan description we spoke of earlier is 'the two ends of a whore', or even 'a whore's melt' on Erneside.

'Let the hare sit,' says the cautious fellow who wants to see 'the way that the cat jumps' before making up his mind.

You know, I was 'put to the pin of my collar' to get that many Fermanagh sayings, and to tell you the truth, I'm flummoxed after all.

Fights and Threats

THE COOLEENS and Lalor-Black Mulvihills, Caravats and
Shanavests, Three and Four Year Olds, Pudding Lane Boys,
Hens and Magpies were old Irish faction fighters who banded
together to fight on behalf of an injured party, or for the
'crack', which might well be of the skull. Women brought
stones in their aprons for the menfolk to 'peg' at their oppo-
nents before they came to close quarters.

Fighting words heard today do not date back to the nineteenth century, some of them come from the tragic people of a
troubled city who still allow themselves a humorous phrase or
two.

'If you fall, don't take time to get up but run on.'

'I'll lambaste you, so I will.'

'Were they fighting over the dog?' 'Oh, there's more to it
than that, as the monkey said looking at his stitched tail that
was chopped off and settled again.'

'He got thumped.'

'I'll bate the livin' daylights out of you.'

'I'll split you.'

'I'll open you with a belt and you won't know what hit
you.'

'I'll destroy you.'

'I'll give you a fistful of your teeth.'

'I'll bury you.'

'I'll give you a dig in the ribs.'

'He hit me a woeful dunt.'

'I'll upend you.'

'I wouldn't face up to that fellow for all the tea in China.'

'I'll cut the socks off you.'

'I'll hit you between the eye and the ear where you can't lick it.'

'A pair of men were fighting like two cats (or like tinkers):

'"I'll ate you without salt," threatened one.

'"You and what army? I'd upend ten like you," came the confident reply.

'"I'll have you know I had medals for boxing," said the first.

'"Aye, when Moses was in the fire brigade." At that, the first fellow hopped off your man and be the hokey, man, but didn't he beat him good-looking. Honest to God, he massacred him!

'Well, he gave him such a goin' over that babes wouldn't look at the same side of the street as him after that.'

Weapons were found in the homes of some Belfast men. The remark was made: 'They haven't a leg to stand on with all the arms found on them!' 'Off they were took in a saccharin tank,' said a woman. The same lady once said that she was 'afraid to take a parcel down off the shelf in case it went up!'

'Sally and me fell out' – there was nobody hurt, for falling out is simply breaking off being on speaking terms. Soon, however, something would happen to 'set the cat among the pigeons' and 'the threats would fly':

'Dip your head under the sea at Ballymoney!'

'Dip yours twice but bring it up onest (once)!'

'Go and take a running jump at yourself!'

'Ah, go and boil your head in a pot and shake the bones out of it!'

'I'll settle your hash for you!'

'You're a right go by the road. But you're all noise and little wool as the man said shaving the pig.'

'I'll give you Paddy Ryan's supper (a beating).' Either

tiring of the argument or fearing the worst would come to the worst and she might 'get a going over', discretion might be shown by retirement and a derogatory, 'I wouldn't dirty my hands on you'.

'The back of my hand to you' is a refusal to shake hands.

'Swearing a hole in a pot' is frequent swearing.

'I'll leave you with a lump on your lug that you'll have to take to a blacksmith!'

'You'll be sorry you riz me!'

My advice to recipients of such threats is to grab an ash plant, hit him and be done with it. 'Bury' him (strike him), and when prosecuted say, 'I had nothing in my hand but my fist!'

Yes, the 'loaded butt' (the whip-handle laden with lead used along with *bataí madaí*, the *ailpín* or the *cipín* in the faction fights of old) may have disappeared from the Irish scene, but tales of bravado are still rife:

'I poleaxed him.'

'He went down like a ton of bricks.'

'He went out like a light after the beltin' I gave him.'

'He was nearly *bás gan sagart* (dead without having a priest).

'I dar you hot me' was a challenge heard in many a school playground.

'Hold my coat and let me at him' might well have been the reply. This might cause a coward to 'cut his stick', 'clear off with himself', beat a hasty retreat.

Rows between husband and wife are treated with more reverence when spoken about. 'She gave him down the banks', or, 'She gave him how's your father' because he told her she was 'as tight as a fish's arse and that's water-tight'. (The anatomical reference to the fish conveyed meanness.) 'Shut your face, you thunderin' galoot,' she shouted at him.

'Ah, don't get your knickers in a knot, woman!'

With that , she 'hit him a haymaker' and threatened to do him in. She told him she wished she could 'get shut of him for once and for all'.

'Are you thick or just plain dumb with your monster-piece

of a nose on you?' The insults would start flying at this stage:

'Oh, as the twig is bent so is the tree inclined. Your auld lad was no better than you.'

Bringing the partner's family into the conversation was guaranteed to 'hot things up'. 'I don't know why I ever took this gold ring from you,' she roared, pointing to her wedding ring.

'Nor me neither. A curtain ring would have fitted your big "glaum" just as handy.' ('Glaum', used for a big awkward hand but more often as the verb 'glauming' – awkwardly handling.)

'My face was my fortune,' she declared.

'Yes indeed. And it ran into a big round figure,' he answered back. And so it went on.

'Fight? Jaysus, sure he wouldn't bate snow off a rope.'

'I cotch him at my turf so I hot him on the beak.'

'Every man for himself, as the ass brayed, and he leppin' into the flock of hens.'

'It's a mortal tough fight.'

'I'm black out with her.'

'He wasn't worth a dam at the gladiatin'.'

'Hello, hard chaw!'

'Shu' up or I'll lep through you!'

'A cat has leave to look at a king, head!'

'You might have whiskers but I'm not wearin' a crown, mate.' A blow is struck.

'Here. Hit somebody your own size. You wouldn't hit your match, as Mick Sheehy said to the fox.'

'You're as windy as the Sally Gap.' (Windy is cowardly.)

'And you're all blow like Tom Ryan after the onions.' Another punch is thrown, accompanied by the instruction:

'Put that in your pipe and smoke it. God, I'm blue-mouldy for a beating. (Bragging. The opponent is much 'scrawnier' – a 'bit of an old weed', in fact.) Blazes Kate! I'll tear you asunder.'

'Do you ever quit chawin' the rag?' – giving abuse.

'Don't forget to bring a shovel.' (To dig the grave.) The big lad strikes again. 'There's the coward's puck for you' – a blow to goad the coward into responding.

'Keep your craags to yourself' – hands.

'Ah, you're always gaatching around ('shaping' – posing pretentiously). You're a blooming heartscald (a torment). If my brother was here he'd beat you hollow.'

'What are you talkin' about? None of your lot would beat a kettle-drum.'

'Tom would leather you. That's for sure.'

And so it goes on. The threats, the fear of being beaten or of appearing afraid. The almost sacred duty of the Irish to be bigger and tougher and stronger than the other.

> *I leathered him with my shillelagh*
> *For he trod on the tail of my coat.*

Yes, a gentle step on one's coat warrants a sound thrashing.

Remember Synge's *Playboy of the Western World*? A hero because he killed his father! A 'belt of a loy' on the poor man's skull (imagined), and villagers were agape and women falling over the great ape of a fellow who acted so!

'He was a made man, was up stacks, wouldn't call the queen his aunt.'

'There's *míle* murder (murder a thousandfold – general mayhem) going on outside. If I catch that fellow I'll knock the priest's share (soul) out of him.' This might be a father's threat concerning a fighting son – while he glanced out the window to make sure the son was winning!

The father is secretly hoping the big lump of a son will 'smather' the fellow he's fighting with – will make 'smush' or 'small bits' of him, in fact.

Fair means or foul, it's all the one with him. The lad can lash out with his 'big spaug' (large foot) into the opponent's 'snitch' (face) and disfigure him, so he can. There would be 'wigs on the green' if herself thought the father was thinking along these lines, of course.

'But, by the hokey, there's a crowd comin' to assist the

other fellow. Oh, but look at that – my fellow taking them out of a face. Be the holy fly, but this is great. Begod, is he wiltin' a bit, I wonder? Maybe I should go out and give him a hand. Still and all that would be encouraging the spleen (split, row).

'Maybe I'd better leave well enough alone and not be meeting trouble half way. He's well able to look after himself anyhow. He wouldn't be a son of his father's if he wasn't.'

'He'll give it to them, hot and heavy.'
'He'll make laneways through them.'
'He'll devour them.'
'The fish swims dead or alive and so does the soul.'

So let me close my trap on fighting and fights for it is dangerous to be talking about such things. Idle gossip can turn to informing and you know what they say of that: 'More Irish graves were opened by the mouth than by the spade.'

Games and Sporting

FOR RAMBLING, for roving, for football or sporting. Thady Quill was the personification of a sport-loving people who have a unique way of expressing their vehemence or praise for a performer.

'Let it in around Maggie's kitchen!' they shout at a forward, but when he misses (the square) and it goes wide, they say, 'There's plenty of room for it there', or simply, 'As wide as a gate'. If a player has trouble turning they say: 'He'd want a field to turn in.'

A county team that looks promising early in the season receive the rating: 'There's an All-Ireland in them.'

If a referee shows any trace of partiality the call comes: 'Put on a jersey, ref.'

Sweepers to strikers at the corner of the box are common in soccer.

A young boy got his face dirty playing football at school. When the teacher chastised him for not washing his face before coming into class, he said: 'But I did sir. But me ma says I dry a bad colour.'

At a boxing match, if the contestants are not 'mixing it', the crowd often start lilting the 'Blue Danube' waltz in derision. 'Watch out, the ref. is watching', or 'It's not a mortaler (mortal sin) to touch, you know' also suit that occasion. 'I'll hold you a gallon of Inishowen to a gallon of Roscrea' conveys a wager, perhaps by the fellow who would 'bet on two flies going up a wall'.

'Well, we gave them who began it in the final.'

'That other crowd didn't know what hit them, but do you

know what I'm going to tell you, I had a feeling in my water we were going to win all the time.'

'Unlucky! If I bet on a duck to swim, it would drown.'

Exaggerations storm the world of sport too: 'He was catching seagulls out of the sky'; 'You wouldn't bate them with a big stick'; 'He laid out six of them an' he goin' for the goal'.

'He thinks the safe period is half-time against the Rockies.'

'Tom says he has a safe pair of hands.' – 'Yes. But he forgot the combination.'

'He kicked a Garryowen and there was snow on it when it came down.'

A fisherman says he 'got stuck in' a fish.

A card-player says he 'should have hit the Queen with his spade'.

From Tongues of Tinkers

NOWADAYS, FOLK like to call them itinerants, travellers and other more acceptable names, but the McDonaghs, Nevins, Coffeys, Wards, Powers, Cashes, Joyces, Connors and other families that still wander around the countryside take no umbrage at being called *tinkers*. Comfortable caravans have replaced many-wheeled, horse-drawn vehicles which are now rented at high prices to tourists, but many tinkers still live in canvas tents, often having ingenious chimneys allowing a fire within.

However, they did now always have tents. The travelling people once depended on the goodness of Ireland's country people to provide shelter in barns, sheds or haylofts. Then, an Irish tinker, Arthur McDonagh, was imprisoned in England and when he was released he joined a band of gypsies and noted their cheap mode of erecting tentage upon crude frames. He brought back the idea to Ireland, advising his people never to be dependent on settled people again. The first Irish tinkers' camp is said to have been erected near Boyle, Co. Roscommon.

Some tinkers claim that they can steal without committing sin on Good Friday, because a tinker stole one of the four nails prepared to crucify Jesus. They are a religious people and believe fervently in 'Dhaluin' (God) and the 'Naderum of the Dhaluin' (His mother). 'Gillies' and 'gillie-goolies' they call gypsies because they haven't the Faith. A tinker once blinded the 'midil' (the devil, pronounced *meedil*), perhaps by hitting him a belt of his 'mosuir' (hammer) in the 'lurc' (eye), and so no tinker will ever go to hell.

Tinkers used often get 'a tarisuin boot' on an article –

almost the same way as his metropolitan hard-up friend would hock it. They would get a half-crown ('tarisuin', pronounced *tawershoon*) by handing over a piece of harness, for example. Who would ever think that 'Srikel gev his lorc to Stoffirt for Sraterine's grainne' would mean that Michael gave his cart to Pat for Catherine's ring?

All these words are from the language of the tinkers, known as 'Cant'. The pronunciation is the same as Gaelic.

Tinkers once conned many an unsuspecting swain with a 'gladar box'. This contraption was a type of mould into which the tinker would pour melted solder to demonstrate to his intended victim how he could double his money. By sleight of hand, the tinker would make it appear that a genuine coin which he planted was the result of his manufacturing in the gladar box. He would convince the watcher and would then ask him for a large number of coins to be doubled. He would also ask for a few days in which to perform the task – in which time he would be 'at the back end of nowhere' or 'the back of beyonds' – the far end of the country perhaps.

The poor victim would be 'still looking' – stupefied at being caught.

'Don't repeat a word of what I'm telling you, reader, for you'd never *grani* who might be *glorin* (you'd never know who might be listening). If I do hear that you repeated a word *be the Dhalum seek sudil but I'll corib your jeel achusc* (by the good God almighty, I will kill you tonight).

'But come inside and have *a trip of scoitchelp with a nork of inoc libis by the chera* (a cup of tea with a pinch of sugar by the fire). Meet the *gatera* (father) and the *sicer siscars* (three sisters) and *od cams* (two sons).

'*Salc the inoc of the rodus* (take the latch off the door), *scop it* (open it), *misli isturt* (go in) and find a *losc* to *gushie ishirt* (stool to sit upon).

'Don't mind if the *beoir is gotin the goya the miscin* (wife is suckling the baby) but *tolsc my jeel* (follow me).

'I'm after havin' a provin' match this day on the top of her (I had a fight with a man because of his making up to her).

Now sit down there and I'll tell you a yarn about a *Gillie Smith* (Ulster tinker).

'The *ripoch* was *beoir* (whore was pregnant) and she went to the *siskar* (doctor). The *siskar* thought she needed a laxative but the woman, then living in Clare, said that she wanted to have her *losport* (bastard) in Belfast, and her only ailment was her pining, for her heart was in Northern Ireland.

'Slightly aggrieved at his diagnosis being ignored, the doctor testily replied, "I don't give a tinker's dam where your heart is, but your bowels have to be in the Free State, you *mongadan* (fool).

'Well, if you saw the *gredin* (face) of her!

'"*Tasp gut may luber you* (the curse of God on you)," she roared, "*nurch will suni milse* (you'll see me again), and I'll have the *shades* (gardaí) with me next time."

'"Away with you, *nacer* (tinker)," said the doctor.

'"*Cradi* your *pi* (shut your mouth)," said the woman.

'Well, the two of them kept on rantin' and ravin' at each other until they were both *corribed* with the *goop* (perished with the cold), so in the heel of the hunt she took the laxative and headed back for her *luban* (tent) in the *addis* (campsite). There she sat beside the *tober* (road), *salced* the *chimmas* and *gretid a buri cherra* (took the sticks and made a good fire), and in no time at all she had forgotten the incident and was bidding "*Laisiuil talosc*" (Fine day) to everyone who was passing – which soon included herself, if you get what I mean!'

'*Goti milse* a *melk* o' *feha*' – give me a bit of meat.

'*Nolsc* your *miltog*' – wash your shirt.

'*Buicead* the *merrigin*' – hold on to the box.

'You're *mislien* out of your *liart*' – you're out of your mind.

'We didn't *suni* his *jeel* in a *stoffie tuirisc*' – we didn't see him for a long time.

'She *bogs lospied* to *Gisan*' – she gets married to John.

'*Searc* your *inoc*' – cut your hair.

'*Curlim a naisin*' – I will sleep here.

'*Tari* in your own tongue and the *glocotes* won't *grani*' – speak in your own tongue and the police will not understand.

'I'll *suni* your *jeel stoffie*' – I'll see you quickly, or soon.

There is great camaraderie among tinkers. They look after their own with a loyalty that is hard to come by in these times. They congregate at weddings, funerals and courts, and they will even make collections to pay the defence counsel if one of their clan is in trouble. They will fight with members of another clan if provoked – but not 'at the drop of a hat' (at the least opportunity) as many believe.

The trade of the tinsmith has been made all but extinct by the arrival of cheap plastic. The tinker's dam, referred to earlier, was a tiny piece of material used to block very small holes in cans. His solder was his *gradar*. *Stan* was his tin. He had '*tom* and *bini sharcurs*' (big and small scissors), a '*grunsa*' (hoop) for general use, and a '*luscan*' which was a special hoop for a tin-can, his main product.

✄ ✂

The tinker won't 'say no to a *scringan rillye*' (refuse alcoholic drink) when he's *searcing* (cutting). His '*steamer* is *taned* with *spunch*' (pipe is full of tobacco). He might 'take *stall* in a *cena*' (take lodgings in a house) if his work will last a while, and if the *gairead* (money) is good. He will probably lie in the *scibollin* (shed) and make his '*n 'geaccas, srittles, guppas, glorogs* and *srishes*' (tin cans, kettles, pots, teapots and tin basins) on the *caideogs* (flags of the floor) as he sits on a *losc* (stool) by the *lub* (chimney). While employed, he might take an old '*gruffan, miltog strides* or *halor*' (coat, shirt, trousers or cap) from the man of the house, and perhaps an odd *peck* (loaf), piece of *ide* (butter), pinch of '*weed, lascan* or *grunim*' (tea, salt or oatmeal) from the mistress. He might steal '*rumogs* of *cullens* or *innockniabs* or *grutans* from the *ragli*' (eggs, potatoes, turnips, onions from the garden) and eat them with '*lush*' (porter) for his *gricheir* (dinner).

A tinker was wandering home *scimeis* (drunk) one *dolimi* (night). He crossed a *sark* (field) and crossed a *srat* (gate) into a

graveyard by mistake. He fell into a grave that was opened for
a burial on the morrow. He was feeling *gami* (bad), and after
two unsuccessful attempts at getting out of the grave he lay
down moaning and groaning. Later on in the *dolimi* (night),
another wandering drunk came the same way, heard the
lugin (crying), arrived at the grave and look-ed down at the
tinker.

'What's wrong with you, *feen* (man)?' he asked.

'I'm cold,' replied the tinker from below.

'Well why did you kick all the clay off yourself then?'
asked the drunk.

'*Mutas* is *shurrien anurt*' – Tom is hurrying now.

'The *cripach* will *corib* the *inocs*' – the cat will kill the mice.

'That *misleor granies* the *tober achunsc*' – that journey-man
knows the road this night.

'I *grani* it *burier* than him' – I know it better than him.

'That's a *laisiuil talosc*!' – that's a fine day.

'There was *robbiniuc* in the *hawrum*' – there was rain in the
morning.

'*Lush* your *gricheir*' – eat your dinner.

'*Srani* has the *griffin binni* of her *lasun naderum*' – Mary has
her grandmother's petticoat.

'If I get the *dorahoig* in *aise* I'll *misli aharum* (if I can stay here
for the night, I'll leave in the morning) – No! Well the *tasp* may
lub you (bad luck to you). All right. I'm off. But remember,
every dog has his day and I'll be back when I see better days
and I'm telling you, I'll take you down a peg or two then …
and don't threaten me with that *nuggle* (gun). I'll have the law
on you. Worse still, I'll get the Bould Boy Reillys after you.
That crowd would *bate* the *mutogs* off you (beat the socks off
you).'

Connaught

TO HELL or to Connaught – The Cromwellian curse made the land beyond the Shannon an Irish-speaking enclave, and at the turn of the eighteenth century the province was almost entirely Irish-speaking. From the fascination and charm of Galway Bay and beyond to wild Achill and Sligo's 'Yeats Country', Connaught boasts of an Irish-speaking tradition that forced even the foreigner to learn the tongue, for there could be no communication with the oppressed otherwise. In 1823, the mother-tongue was spoken almost exclusively in the 'City of the Tribes' – Galway.

Because of its very Irishness, then, Connaught may not figure greatly in this book of sayings and expressions, as it is from her still-flowing fountain of a lyrical and lovely language that most of the sayings come, and it would be foolish to attempt to extract more than a tincture from a rich source.

We start in the Roscommon-Leitrim-Sligo area. The Roscommon 'Sheep-Stealers', the Leitrim 'Quacks' and the 'Sly Goers' – almost all of them abide by a verse I picked up there:

> *Who knows the most has least to say*
> *But he who knows the least will talk and talk away.*

However, the persons bearing nicknames like 'Plubber' (*plobaire*), 'Sonny Bawn' (*bán*), 'Ropeen', 'Hughie's Barney' and 'Marwawn' (*Máire Bhán*), still socially and economically almost self-sufficient, bear testimony to the area's claim to a particular place in our history. A claim based on a fortitude and a will to survive on subsistence farming of a small holding and to preserve from the past some of the healthy ways of living.

'Ignorance would burst through a rock,' they say. 'Ah will you sthop,' is the remark when disbelief is expressed.

Cord is called 'thumb twine', and a bullock might be acclaimed as: 'a fine baste. He have humps on him like a camel.' 'He gave it tight to her' means 'He gave her a good run for her money', or 'He ran her close'.

'That's a bit thick' is said if something is considered unfair.

'It was good with them, surely' – they were entertaining.

'It isn't six o'clock with him at all' – he doesn't get up at six – but much later, or earlier.

''Twas at death's door with her' – she almost died.

It is the construction of the spoken word that makes the expressions from this area.

'She was killed with a bull' – she was gored to death. (They were not put down together!)

'No one can open his gob with you' – you talk so much that nobody else can get a word in edgeways.

'Don't bring the evening with you' – the speaker demands a return home before twilight.

> *Convince a man against his will,*
> *He's of his own opinion still.*

It was not against my will that I was convinced of the authenticity of the claim that there lived in Ballyfarnum at the end of the poverty-stricken last century families called Slack, Slow, Needam and Want.

A 'trindle' is a wheel of a wheelbarrow; a 'sprunge' is a scrawny beast; a 'skib' is a flat potato-basket; a 'gibbadaun' is a giddy person; and a tramp in 'duggins' would be in rags. A wall between two holdings is called a 'cly-thoran' (*cladh teorann*). Potatoes cooked on a fire at the headland when the harvesting of the crop was taking place tasted as sweet as they sounded – 'brunoge' or 'brohoge'.

'The less I praise you, the less I lie.'

'The Lord will open a gap for him', or 'God never closes one gate but he opens another', and, 'God between us and all harm' – ejaculations and sayings from people of a deep faith!

'I was pushing an open door' – I had no problem.

'There was lashin's and lavin's' – there was plenty.

'She had too much mileage up' – she had knocked around with a fair few men.

'Don't bother your time', or 'Don't put yourself out' – often said in contempt at a refusal to help.

'Are you right there, Michael, are you right?' – words addressed to the driver of a train in another part by a man of great wit and nostalgia – Percy French. Born in Clooneyquinn, Co. Roscommon, Percy was a painter, an engineer, a poet, an actor and 'a bit of a divil'. But he was a lovable 'divil', as his songs 'Eileen Óg', or 'Phil the Fluter' ('batterin' the floor'), or 'Whistlin' Phil McHugh' demonstrate so well.

During his student days, Percy was often keeping the wolf from the door by acting and singing. On a wet day he might declare that it was 'a good job the right side of the house was out'. Of the many parties he attended, he might announce that 'the world and his wife were there', and having charged a hefty fee for entertaining at one of them, he might remark: 'That will soften their cough for them.'

Percy himself said that Mrs Cafferty was 'leppin' like a hare'. His songs sold 'like hot cakes', and other troubadours were 'only in the ha'penny place with him'. But he 'tried to bring every side with him' (he attempted to do everything), and it was 'clear as the driven snow' that he was 'burning the candle at both ends'.

'Take the floor – go round the house and home by the dresser!' – Not encouragement to commandeer a bit of parquet and sneak it into a residence via the tailor's, but an invitation to dance at a 'hoolie'. Phil the Fluter with 'a young slip of a thing' was 'happy as Larry' even though he didn't 'make as good a fist' of the dancing as he did of the fiddling. Telling the 'gaherla' that she was 'a cure for sore eyes' and she thinking he was as old as the hills. She 'ditched' him, of course, but off with him then sniffin' after one of the Misses Brady that had come in their private ass and car – working on the premise that 'a half a loaf is better than no bread'.

Oh, but I shouldn't be running down those Bradys – neither with my car nor my pen! Aren't they as snug as a bug in a rug in their small holding not a stone's throw away from the town? And haven't they the grass of a goat and a cow into the bargain? The pair of them are like peas in a pod, and if they never go to Church, Mass or meeting itself, aren't they of the old stock? – every one of them as straight as a die.

Leitrim, Roscommon, Sligo – who better to justify an attempt at presenting the dialogue of the people there than their most illustrious adopted son, W.B. Yeats? –

> Better go down upon your marrow-bones
> And scrub a kitchen pavement, or break stones
> Like an old pauper, in all kinds of weather;
> For to articulate sweet sounds together
> Is to work harder than all these.

In Coolooney, the River Unshin joins the Owenmore and together they press on through the valley between the spurs of Sliabh Daeane and Sliabh Gamh. Atop Daeane is the house of the Cailleach Bhearra. 'Now there was a right old rip! In fact she was a flute of an old one – a cod, no good. Hard as flint she was and as bald as a turnip, some say. She was as slippery as an eel's waistcoat, and had a nose on her like a pin-pointer. She was as lonely as a church-mouse up there on the hill, and she without chick nor child. Lucky, for she was so crooked that if she swallowed a knitting needle 'twould come out a corkscrew.'

'Never a fair in Keadue or a court in Cootehall' – Before the advent of the cattle-mart, when fairs were held in towns and villages throughout Ireland, many attempts were made to hold a fair in Leitrim's village of Keadue. So too with the village of Cootehall nearby. Attempts to hold a court there always met with failure.

'Begob, but you're a right schemer. You're always up to something.'

'Will I give you a pound for the spuds? What a fool I'd be!'

'That's a quare auld yoke'; 'That's a funny contraption of a thing'.

'You wouldn't want to open your mouth there. The two of them's terrible thick' – Say nothing to either of them. They're very close friends. 'Thick' can also mean 'huffed', and 'a thick' is the same as 'a lug', only more boorish.

'A sup of sugeen' is a drop of water in which oatmeal has been soaked. It was often drunk by haymakers to quench their thirst.

'Causha-pooka' (*cáisc na púca*) is a fungus found in the open fields and its name means 'the pooka's cheese'. The pooka, of course, was a phantom hare – perhaps the devil – and children went out with the pooka on Hallow's Eve. Children also had a rude name for the fungus. If wind broken by a bull has substance, then there's no reason why we shouldn't believe the children!

'That fellow is no good – there's bad in him somewhere.'

'Oh, I don't know. He has a good name down around Mohill.'

'Small wonder. Every fox has a good name in his own parish.'

That piece of conversation ends with a saying based on an old theory that a fox did not kill fowl in the area where it lived but wandered the length and breadth of the neighbouring barony at his thieving.

To tell you the truth, I think that old talk is 'as I roved out'

or 'all me eye', or 'to be taken with a grain of salt'. It is
'eyewash' – untrue. But perhaps I'm wrong not to believe it. If
so, then tell me that 'one fool is enough in any parish'.

Between Newtowngore and Ballinamore, in the barony of
Carrigallen, lies the townland of Garadice. A girl from that
area married the son of a Dromahair man, 'fond of the drop'.
The old man went visiting the couple in Garadice, a place he
had never been before. He found it very remote and back-
ward, and he got no porter, let alone spirits, while he was
there.

On his return from the place, he made a bee-line for the
pub and his cronies asked him what he thought of Garadice.
'Well, I'll tell you this,' said the old man, 'if Paradise is anything like Garadice, I pray to God I'll never see it.'

'Three bad things in the house: a scolding wife, a smoking
chimney and a screaming child.'

'Give me a dreas of that' means give me a small quantity
of that. In Clare, we see, the term refers to three turns of the
churn handle to comply with the custom. (Also spelt 'drass'.)

The 'ludeen' (*lúidín*) is a common name for the little finger. Not so common are 'Thumbbui' for the thumb and 'Lis-
bui' for the first finger.

In Clare, the second, third and small fingers were one time
called 'Longman, Jiggedy and Jack Dandy' respectively.

'A man is never as alone as in the middle of the bog.'

'The rain was beltin' out.'

'Ah, the dead arose!' or 'Ah, the hard and the wild!' – said
when a very welcome but unexpected guest arrives.

'There's a proposal in the Senate to drain the Shannon' –
think of it!

'Stop trying to take a rise out of me' – stop trying to make
a fool out of me.

'It's straight on after the next turn. You don't have to ask
the road.'

'She was wooden (thick, dense), woolly (confused), as thin as a rail and as sore as a briar (cross). There are some who say she was mad out or as daft as a halfpenny watch.

'She would put the come-hither on you (she would upset your plans), but sure, even if the old battle-axe was a right pain in the neck (bore) and an old haybag, she failed something terrible in the end and changed from being a heap (stout) and as round as a hoop into someone that a spoon of water would drown (small).'

In Sligo, they say, 'as thick as an ass' instead of the more usual 'as thick as a ditch'. 'As stubborn as an ass' it is too – the mule is exonerated in Sligo.

'As dry as a pinch of snuff.'

'As ugly as sin' – and 'lonesome looking' is ugly too.

'He had a red nose on him like a cherry' – he drank.

'He had a belly on him like a harvest frog.'

'He's as cute as Cut the Bags.'

'He had a head on him like a boiled pike.'

'She went as green as a leek and suddenly went out like a light' – she became a green colour and then fainted.

'She's high'; 'She's flitterin'' – she's in a temper.

'He did the dirty' – he acted meanly. (Also 'did *it* dirty'.)

'I'd sleep on a harrow but I'll be rearin' to go in the morning' – I'm very tired but will be full of beans in the morning.

A Sligo woman mourned the passing of the days when potatoes ('spuds', 'poppies') were plentiful: 'God be with the days when I couldn't see the auld fella (husband) across the table with the hape (heap) of skins.' But 'sit lightly' (be prepared for changes), old woman! There's better days ahead!

Perhaps some young man thought 'live horse and you'll get grass' encouraged a nag to go to POT or become a drug *naggict*! Or maybe this fellow was the type that 'would promise you the birds in the bushes, but go out and catch them yourself'. He might have 'higher tanners' prices' and might 'skin a flea for a halfpenny and sell its hide for a penny', unlike other countrymen who would be content at their first sale. Of course, the chap might believe that 'a crooked loaf makes a straight belly'. 'It's a long road that has no turning', however, and 'when the wheel has gone full circle' (when he arrives back where he started), he might realise that 'the mills of God grind slowly but they grind extremely well'. In the meantime, he is 'come a day, go a day, God send Sunday' (careless), not like 'his nibs' at the other end of the parish who 'still has his Confirmation money' (or First Communion money, depending on his degree of tightness or meanness). With this fellow, 'every penny is a prisoner'.

But who knows these days? He has 'as much money as would sink a ship, and he owes as much as would sink two' is a common observation. Such a fellow is often 'like a cow chewing turnips' (has bad manners at table) when he sits down to a meal.

> *Fáilte romhat minic a thig,*
> *Is mór an trua nach minic nach dtig*
> *Nach dtagann chomh minic le minic a thig.*

These lines lament the inevitable arrival of the unwelcome guest and the infrequency of the visit from the pleasant person – 'minic a thig' the former, and 'minic nach dtig' the latter.

'All her geese are swans' – she boasts.

'She's like "lanagh mo chroidhe's" cat (also "allanagh mo chroidhe's" dog) – a bit of the road with everyone' – refers to the person who tries to have many friends.

'There's a donkey in every job' – this is often said regarding the very hard-working committee-member who gets little thanks and less praise.

Leitrim, Galway and Mayo, as well as Sligo lay some claim to the origin of the saying 'It takes the biscuit' because the modern confection was preceded by a cake. But let me explain:

A number of theories exist about cake dances which seemed to be rituals held with a cake made to have signs of the Zodiac raised upon it – a type of Ouija-cake, by all accounts!

At a 'prinkum' (soirée, 'hoolie', celebration), a cake was placed on an upturned churn-dash and stuck in the ground and danced around. In some locations there is no reference to the signs, but a shebeen-keeper (proprietor of an unlicensed liquor house) sent a cake to the dancers outside in the hope that he would encourage them to disperse. Yet other references are to cakes eaten at 'patterns' or 'patron-days' around holy wells. One thing is common to all accounts, however: the best dancer took the cake. But if he did, the poor fellow also 'took the sway' and had to treat everybody 'come Hell or high water', 'no matter what way the cat jumped' (at all costs).

8 September was *Lá 'le Muire Mór* (*Lá Fhéile Muire Mór* –Big Lady Day, the Feast of Our Lady's birthday), and Erris resounded to the music as bargains were made and dances were danced, and he who took the cake there became really famous. The couples who took the floor – 'riz the dust' might be more accurate – at Erris were only the best, the Almighty best in the land. They were as sprightly on their feet as bantams and were invited to dance upon *leac na tine* at every '*céilí* house' for the following year.

It was normally the prerogative of the man of the house to dance on the *leac na tine*, but it was customary to extend to those who took the cake at Erris on *Lá 'le Muire Mór* this privilege if they 'made a *cuairt*' (visited).

The *leac na tine* was a large flagstone in front of the fire under which were placed old pot-ovens. These allowed an amplified sound to come from the foot-tapping of those who danced upon the *leac*. Pot-ovens were low iron pots which were used for roasting, baking and the like – what would be done in an oven nowadays.

An 'afterthought' is a child born a long time after the main section of a family. This is a modern expression, for the non-family-planning-days of old never occasioned such a child. Be that as it may, a woman was accused of murdering such a child and of putting its body beneath the *leac na tine*, for its skeleton was discovered there. The woman was acquitted, however, on the grounds that she was too old to bear a child at fifty-four, and that it was impossible for a child to survive birth into such impoverished conditions as existed in the particular household.

When the *meitheal* (working party) came in from the hayfield after their day's work and were fed and foddered, they took their drink and stretched themselves and prepared for the nights's *cuartaíocht* (visiting) when other less tired feet would dance before the fire for their entertainment. All the better if the feet were those of dark or auburn *cailíní* (girls, now universally alluded to as 'colleens'). For then a man might 'let the weight of the world drop from him' (discard his worries) as he marvelled at the wonders of the God above that could make such sweetness as woman, while lissom young life cavorted the more, knowing full well the eyes that were upon her and knowing even better that she possessed what could please the same eyes.

The women would call her a 'brazen hussy', a 'strap' – especially the ugly women! The ugliest would probably call her 'the village bicycle' after the invention of the said mode of transport. But the men – well, they'd 'say more with their looks than could a thousand words express better', but what it would all boil down to would be the fact that the girl was 'easy on the eye', 'a bit of all right', 'by no manner of means any way plain', 'nice to be pullin' a cord with' (courting), and that a fellow would need to be a 'quare eejit' not to want to be 'great with her'.

If she had 'little or nothing on her itself', what matter? For wasn't there 'a rake of auld ones' 'dressed to the nines' in the corner that 'wouldn't be any good to man or beast'. Many a man there remembered smacking the lassie's bottom playfully as she developed, and thought to himself, 'When I helped her wind the clock, I might as well hear it strike'. And even if he was 'as straight a man as ever drew breath', he couldn't help thinking as he looked at her 'all dolloped in powder and paint', how he would like to 'trot her' a couple of times. 'No more beatin' around the bush,' he thought as he leapt up to ask her to dance.

'A thin breeze without tonight!'

'Mmmm.'

'What has you so cranky?'

'Mmm – ah, nothin'.'

'I wouldn't mind a bit of a conversation.'

'A pity about you!'

'Or a bit of somethin' else – with a backside on you like two rabbits tryin' to get out of a sack.'

'The cheek of you.'

'The cheeks of you. What has the pint sour (what's wrong)?'

'You needn't think I'll gallop for every go by the road!'

'Who said you would?'

'You wouldn't want to.'

'This is neither right nor lucky.'

'What isn't?'

'This class of carry-on – not talking or anything.'

'Who's not talking?'

'Are you making game of me?'

'Now you're in a right nonplush. You don't know whether you're comin' or goin'.'

'You think you're the rale Ali Daly, don't you?'

'If you knew what way I was takin' you, you wouldn't call the Pope your aunt.'

'You think you're horrid smart'.

'Well, you'd need to be up early in the morning to catch me out.'

'Ah, there's more than one way of drowning a cat.'

'Where did you get the watch?'

'Ah, it goes back to my grandfather' (My grandfather owned it one time).

'When? – next week?'

'There's no sense to this class of tomfoolery.'

'Who put you up to (suggested) asking me to dance?'

'There's neither rhyme nor reason to it.'

'The Lord look down on you, you *amadán* (fool).'

'Look at her (you). Struttin' around like a hen in stubbles.'

'You're fairly full of yourself too (conceited).'

'Bad cess to you!'

'Ach, you're only a *ceolán* (unlikable, silly man).'

'I'll go and look for someone more *cúramach* (thoughtful and kind).'

'I'll find a *giostaire* myself. 'Twould suit me better.' (A *giostaire* is an old man that's young at heart. The girl is 'rising' the fellow.)

'That would be your height (would suit you).'

'Run like the divil from the excise man ... in the Hills of Connemara': the encouraging of the moonshiner making his poteen (*poitín*) in the rocky Galway countryside around Letterfrack or upon the Maamturk and Sheffry Hills; the words of Synge's Playboy whispering across the foothills of Nephin; the proud people of Mayo, Tuam and Tubbernavine where was born the great patriot – Archbishop John MacHale in 1791. Anglo-Irish expressions sound almost profane in their utterance among such a people.

Politics are a little more serious here than elsewhere and it was said of a councillor: 'If it took him a month he would sit in the chambers until his motion was passed.' But politicians must wait and talk and not show signs of haste, for 'when the Lord made time, he made plenty of it'.

Strangers to Galway came under the red bridge – even if they came since the red railway bridge crossing the Oranmore road was demolished! A politician who did not deliver the goods might be told: 'That you may die roarin' like Doran's ass.' If he were not a man of strong character, he would be 'all wind and water like the barber's cat'. If anyone belonging to the politician wore the shirt he was 'a Blueshirt', and I declare to God, I'm not going to get mixed up in that. I'll keep my toe in my pump, run with the hare and hunt with the hounds, and say to all that think ill of me what Michael Collins said to an acquaintance – 'If I'd a mind like yours, I'd drown it in a thimble.'

So, having thus 'rubbed somebody up the wrong way', let me hasten to put down a few words from the records of this area:

'Bosthoon' – a foolish person (*bastún* was also a soft staff made of rushes).

'Smithereens' (*smidiríní*) – tiny pieces. 'I made smithereens of it.'

'Breedoge' (*brídeog*) – the dash of a churn dressed as an effigy of St Brigid and paraded on the eve of the saint's feast-day.

'Bun' – a rabbit's tail (from Irish meaning a stump).

'Cagger' – a travelling man selling bric-a-brac (from Irish, *cágaire* – a hoarder).

'Céilidhe' (or '*céilí*') – a gathering for song dance or 'crack' (*craic*).

'Caubeen' (*cáibín*) – a battered cap.

'Come-All-Ye' – a ballad (most of which start with 'Come all ye....')

'Cleevaun' (*cliabhán*) – cradle.

'Clamp of turf' – rick of turf.

'Crawthumper' – a 'holy Mary' – a hypocrite.

'Hugger-mugger' – 'gostering' – whispering in a corner.

'Gligeen' (*gligín*) – a nitwit.

'Maneen' – 'guban (from *gobán*)' – a boy that is too old for his years, too 'well-up'.

A landlord's son is referred to as a 'half-sir' in Galway. He might be 'as dacent a man as ever wore shoe leather' or he might be 'the two ends of a devil'.

Whether or which, you would be '*ar mhuin na muice*' (on the pig's back), if you met him and kowtowed to him by touching your forelock.

You might do it once too often, however, because 'your

own are those that matter most in the heel of the hunt'. You might get your comeuppance or get 'what's coming to you' if you got too 'well in' with the gentry, no matter how off-hand (casual) they might be with you.

'Come thither the road quickly with me for it was raining today morning (this morning) and before it makes rain again. It was raining ere yesterday (the day before yesterday) too, but it turned out a nice soft day in the end, although there were a few heavy butts to the clouds. Step out on the yard of flagstones (street) and we'll go.

'Now I'm looking for £200 in the meadowing (for meadow) for if I get shut of it soon, I'll get another £100 for the aftergrass (second crop of grass). £200 is the richest price (is a good price) at this time of year.

'Here, take the donkey by the coward (cord, rope). You're like a duck out of water (or a duck in thunder) standing with one hand longer than the other (empty-handed). Wait for me down there at the linnie (back wall of a building that has no gable or high wall of a lean-to) and here's a fistful of gobstoppers (large boiled sweets) to be golloping up (eating hungrily) while you're idle.'

'At the back of God-speed' means in an out-of-the-way place. A careless, fickle person might be called 'Johnny go aisy and his wife, Nancy'. A man with a very thin face 'could kiss a goat between the horns'. If thin all over, he 'got the hind teat of the cow', and he 'was an awful sight altogether' if he 'got the hind teat of a hedgehog'.

'What are you bawlowering about?' is asked of someone shouting. 'He put the caibosh on it' means he really messed it up.

I heard it said in Mayo that there are three kinds of men that do not understand women – young men, middle-aged men and old men. A man with a reputation for women 'would tip a cat going through a skylight', and an awkward fellow would be called 'butterfist'.

'He's as well known as a begging ass for he's always sticking his nose into other people's affairs. He wouldn't get you a
lock of ciarans or a *braoinín* (little drop) of milk, he's that lazy.'
An extra drop of milk for the cat was a 'tilly', and a small
patch of leather sewn on the side of a worn boot was a '*taobh-
ín*'. As cute as a pet fox, as quick as lightning.

'His father hung a bishop' – he's no good.

'He lit the place with curses.'

'All he left me was the slip of a pig' was a complaint after
a will was read. 'Ah, hould your whisht. All your crowd were
up here like flies around a jamjar since he got sick, but you
wouldn't bid us the time of day before that. Go off with you
all for you're never done chewin' the rag.'

'But it's rainin' cats and dogs. Sure you wouldn't put a
dog out on a night like that!'

At wake, wedding or funeral, the sayings fall from the lips
of the men of the West with an ease and a frequency that is
unique. 'How're you aul' sthock?' is a greeting of warmth
from Claddaghside. 'How's your granny for spots?' is a jocose
greeting.

As we watch the sun go down on Galway Bay, however,
we will leave the last word to the Mayo woman who confides
in you about a couple who have been intimate with each other. It is witty in its very simplicity. She nods her head, gathers
her shawl about her shoulders and whispers, 'The tay is wet
there'.

Food and Drink

SAYINGS AND expressions concerning food and drink are plentiful in our land flowing with milk and honey. They are assembled together here for they are common to most parts of the country. Some have already been alluded to as prevalent in a particular area.

'There wasn't what would feed a cricket in it.'

'I got as sick as a dog after her rabbit.'

'Here's a rake of apples for you.'

'You'd want to have an iron constitution to eat it.'

A man with a big appetite has 'a powerful stroke', has 'a mouth on him like the Liffey', or 'has to put his belly up on the table'. If he is impatient waiting for his food he is told: 'A watched pot never boils.' He longs to see the woman of the house 'scald the pot' by heating it with some boiling water before making tea. When he gets his meal, he says, 'The light of Heaven on you'. He takes a heel (crusty end) of bread with his bowl of soup that there is 'eatin' and drinkin' in'. Then to the crubeens (*crúibíns* – pigs' feet) and the 'tilly of buttermilk' and young spuds 'just off the gash' (stalk).

'The woman was handing around the vittles like snuff at a wake, but he was going through it like ♣□✳☆ ! through a goose. Food galore there was and when the ungrateful wretch was finished he stretched out and tore the Joker (broke wind).'

> *Rye bread will do you good,*
> *Barley bread will do no harm,*
> *Wheaten bread will sweeten blood,*
> *Oaten bread make strong your arm.*

'It was but a daisy in a bull's mouth' or 'a midge in the Glen of the Downs' – it was a poor meal.

'You could trot a mouse on the tea' or 'You could stand the spoon in it' – the tea was very strong.

🍵

'Johnny saved his bacon' does not mean that he put some by, but that he had a narrow escape. 'Bully bread' is white soda-bread, and 'prawkeen' is oatmeal soaked in milk.

'God, but she never asked me had I a mouth on me, there was I with the stomach falling out of me. Not even a bit of dip (bread dipped in grease) did she offer me. I damn near whipped (stole) the fry from under her nose when she sat down in front of it smackin' her lips. Well, she wolfed it down like a starved mongrel and only came up for air between every three rashers. Her jaws were going up and down like Waterford Bridge, and the gravy was dripping down on her bib like a leaking pot.

'Then she started into drinking the porter. Well, I tell you this, I never saw anything like it. She would drink the quarter sessions and go back for the courthouse!

'There was I – hanging with the hunger, and I wouldn't have said "No" to a drink either, but there wasn't a gig out of her. In the end, I could stand it no longer, for when she was finished she stretched herself on the *leaba na mbocht* (Bed for a travelling man in the kitchen) and she was like the Mail Boat pulling out with the puffing of her.

'"You mean old haybag," I said.

'"What's atin' you?" she asked.

'"Nothing's atin' me and I'm atin' nothing," says I. And with that I went to the press without even "by your leave", and I made laneways through everything that was there.

'I downed a heel of bread, two onions, made a plate of portermeal (oatmeal and porter) and lowered it too. Before I was finished, I had my whack ('keep' – enough food for a day) out of the targe (unpleasant woman).

'Well, she didn't know what hit her and in next-to-no-time

I had *lán na mhála* (the full of the bag – plenty), buckets of stuff and plenty to spare. I put the caibosh rightly on her when I reached behind the settle (type of bed) and felt for the bottle of poteen that I knew she kept there for medicinal purposes. This was the occasion because it for she was in a nonplush and I had a pain in my face from laughing.'

Drink

> *Whiskey, you're the divil,*
> *You're leadin' me astray;*
> *Over hills and mountains,*
> *And to Amerikay.*
> *You're sweeter, stronger, dacenter,*
> *You're spunkier nor tay;*
> *Oh whiskey you're me darlin', drunk or sober.*

There are more songs about drink, more sayings about drink and more yarns about drink than there are stomachs filled with drink – and that's saying something. If all of the world loves a lover, then all the Irish love a boozer, for haven't you all heard of the Irishman who steps over five naked women to reach a pint of porter?

A man is drunk. He is '*lán 'a mhála*', 'Killarnied', 'under the weather', 'three sheets in the wind', 'elephants', 'bullafance', 'bullhugeous drunk', 'as drunk as a lord', 'as tight as an owl', 'skuttered', 'drim and drool' (nearing sobriety again), 'paralytic', 'jacked', 'stoned', 'spiflicated', 'well cut' ('half cut' if nearly so), 'pissed out of his mind', 'maggoty, mouldy, eejity' (the trio used together, normally), 'doesn't know his religion', 'plastered', 'flyin'', 'his brains is turned to stirabout', 'finding it hard to maintain a relationship with the perpendicular', 'speechless drunk', 'fluthered', 'rightly', 'senseless', 'Cormacked' (also 'Mac Airted'), 'crooked', 'heavy', 'scutri-

fied', 'ossified', 'blotto', 'blind drunk', 'Jimmy-riddled', 'twist-
ed', 'langers', 'screwed'.

The favourite music-hall sketch of the drunken husband
going home to the wife has its Irish equivalent. 'I throw my
hat in the door and if it doesn't come back out, I creep in' –
that ploy was told me by an Inishowen man.

'The missus will make shows,' fears the reveller.

'The jonnick and the gallery are all right but what about
the *rírá* (uproar) when we get home?'

'Herself cut her stick (left home) because I had her heart
scalded from drinking like a fish when there was often no bite
to eat in the house.'

'Look at *mo dhuine* (pronounced 'mogunya') there with the
row of home-rulers lined up in front of him. Pint bottles bear
that patriotic title.

'He fell over his shadow' – he tumbled while he was
drunk.

'There isn't the bate of him in it for knockin' them back
nate' (or 'hard') – he has no equal for drinking raw whiskey,
whiskey that never saw water.

'Will you have a jorum?'

'I thought you'd never ask. Thought you were handcuffed, I did.'

'Two smathans, Joe, and not a deuce less.' (A *smeathán* is a
nip or dram.)

'*Sláinte.*'

'Good luck.'

Taking a drink merely 'to pass himself' (do the right
thing) leads many a man to consume a fair few 'drops of the
craythur'. In no time at all, the drink is flowing like water, for
'a bird never flew on one wing' (said to one who demurs after
one drink).

'My tongue is hanging out for a jar.'

When two drinking pals have more than what's good for them, they are bosom friends as they have to help each other home. It is a case of 'the blind leading the blind' as they stagger along 'as crooked as a dog's pee in the snow'.

Next morning, they 'have heads on them', and one might remark to the other, 'Cripes, Joe, there's bees in me insides.' 'I had more than was good for me last night too,' Joe would reply, 'But sure we'll be dead long enough.'

An old Cork liquor advertisement once announced the quality of :

LITTLE NORA – BOTTLED IN BANDON

The 'holy hour' is the afternoon period of closing for public houses.

'The same again or something similar,' calls the boozer. The call is music in the ears of his mate who says in acclaim: 'You could sing that if you had an air to it.'

'Me life on you, boy.'

'Ah, the old dog for the hard road.'

'That was the father and mother of a hard night.'

'There was no holding him once he had the first one.'

'He took to the stuff and it went through him like a hole in a bucket.'

'Here's mud in your eye.'

'There's no drink like the next drink.'

'He was so full that, if he leaned sideways, he would spill.'

'He would drink whiskey out of a corpse's armpit.'

'Are you drunk?' 'No! I don't drink; I only dip my bread in it.'

'He was hitting the two sides of the road and missing the middle.'

While under the influence of drink, a man drove a new car which had power steering. Halted by a garda, he pleaded, 'It's the power steering, Garda!' The garda replied, 'I know. How many large ones?' (Powers is a brand of Irish whiskey.)

'Bring me drunk; I'm home!'

A man 'had a head' one morning and he struggled into a

pub for a cure. There was nobody in the bar so the owner had left the door to the yard open. A huge St Bernard dog rambled in. The customer took his head out of his hands and found himself staring with bloodshot eyes into the eyes of the huge animal.

He stared for a while and quietly begged, 'You can bite me arse, but for the love of jaysus, don't bark.'

God is good
and the Devil isn't too bad either

THE TITLE of the chapter is a saying attributed to a man who found himself in a dangerous position and, fearing death, he decided to play safe and be 'well in' with both sides if the worst came to the worst.

> *Some say the devil, he lives in Slane*
> *More say he comes from Blarney*
> *But them that's tellin' the truth all say*
> *He joined the British Army.*

The Old Boy, Old Nick, whose prayer book, according to popular belief, is a pack of cards, has a place in many sayings and expressions of the Irish people.

'The devil you know is better than the devil you don't' is a saying used to make somebody content with their lot. 'Speak of the devil and he's sure to appear' is said when somebody appears just as they have been talked about.

The devil is said to have ridden with the 'Killing Kildares', that well-known hunt. What's more, he partook of the stirrup-cup and retired to play cards with the master afterwards. The joker in the pack of cards is associated with the devil and, when the host dropped this card during the course of play, he stooped down to pick it up. Only then did he spy his visitor's cloven feet under the table.

> *A whistling girl and a crowing hen*
> *Will coax the Old Boy from his den.*
> *If right and proper girls remain,*
> *We'll never see Old Nick again.*

God help our dear ladyfolk. Their every curve, ogle, limb and smile brought accusations of being in league with 'himself'.

If accursed by bad luck, the remark is made, 'It's hard to dance with the devil on your back', and doesn't everybody know that 'the devil finds work for idle hands'?

'The devil mend you' is said to somebody who has done something to please one. But good Irish logic makes 'The devil's curse on you' the equivalent to a blessing. 'That fellow is as sharp as the devil's needle' is said of a 'wide boy', an 'eyekie fellow', a 'cute hawk'.

Somebody who is to be pitied is referred to as 'the poor old divil', but a wild girl would be called 'a right divil'.

'The devil's own children have the devil's own luck,' they say of a sharp person who got on well. If in doubt about somebody obliging, the remark would be made: 'Oh, that fellow will do the divil and all till it comes to the push.'

'When you eat with the devil, use a long spoon' – when you have any 'truck' or dealings with rogues, exercise great caution.

'May you be in Heaven an hour before the devil knows you're dead' is our best-known blessing and a fitting introduction to the other side of the coin. God and his heaven are more often included in formal prayers and blessings than within sayings and expressions, but somebody who has had a spell of good fortune is said to have 'a great leg of the Lord'.

Diarmuid Mac Murrough gave the fort at the Rock of Dunamase near Portlaoise to Strongbow as part of a dowry with his daughter, Aoife. Anyhow, there was some celebration after the presentation, and as Strongbow left to lay waste to a village or two before the morning, Mac Murrough is said to have given him the old Irish parting wish, '*Go n-éirí an bóthar leat*'– 'May the road rise with you' is the literal translation, but it only means 'Safe journey'. The wish must have been taken literally, however, for as Strongbow was heading towards Birr via Kinnity, road and countryside rose beneath him, throwing him from his horse.

'God love you' is a type of pitying exclamation. 'God is good' is the expression of all Irish optimists. 'God keep you', 'God be with you', 'God between us and all harm' and 'God only knows' are self-explanatory.

The Irish have a remarkable affection for the Mother of God, and Mary's name is often included in the above ejaculations. The foster-father of Jesus, St Joseph, holds a special place in the prayer-recesses of many an Irish working man, for they believe that this humble carpenter represented the dignity of the common man. An Irishman was extolling the powers of intercession that St Joseph had, and he finished with the remark: 'He's out on his own after the Blessed Virgin.'

An old-fashioned priest admonished a young lady for smoking in public. He spoke to her from his car that had screeched to a halt when the priest saw the offending female.

'Nobody ever saw the Blessed Virgin smoking in public,' said the priest.

'And nobody ever saw her son driving a car at sixty miles an hour,' answered the lady, unabashed.

'Say your prayers and don't fasten the devil' – the advice of many an Irish mother.

Monasterevin was sometimes called 'Evin' for short. Young boys at Kildangan shouted at passing trains: 'Catholics change here for "Evin". Protestants remain seated, the train is going to Cork.'

'The Lord is bringing home the turf' – said in the country when they hear thunder.

'The Lord look sideways on you' is an ill wish.

'God bless the work' is a greeting to workers. 'And you too' is the customary answer.

There is little to eat in the house of God. So, impoverished persons are said to be 'as poor as church mice'.

'God in Heaven!'; 'Good God Almighty!' – exclamations used when shocked.

Two words from the bible dealing with the Passion of Christ are used in swearing and in prayer, and the enunciation decides which. 'Jesus Wept' are the words, but sometimes the phrase 'Jesus wept bitter tears' is used.

'God be good to him' – often used when a man dies, and also used as a general blessing. 'God speed' is said to one setting out on a journey, and 'Holy God!' is an expression of surprise.

The poor sinner that 'never went to Church, Mass or meeting' might make a plea for leniency on the grounds that 'when needs must, the devil drives'. This would mean that he 'was put to it', 'fell foul of the Lord' or adopted his sinful ways because of his poor circumstances.

'That roast is as tough as the devil.'

'The divil blow you.'

'The divil a thing did I get.'

I know of a pair of very religious old ladies who kept a life-sized crucifix in their living room. They were given as a present a modern painting showing the Lord with a huge ear and a large eye. When a visitor came to their house, one of the old ladies showed him this picture and explained that the huge ear and eye symbolised the ear of the Lord that hears all and the eye of the Lord that is all-seeing. The dumbfounded visitor prepared to make some suitable remark when the old lady added, 'Isn't it a very good one of him?'

'May the wind always be at your back and the sun shining warm in your face!'

> *Saint Peter, Saint Paul and Saint Patrick,*
> *All the pictures that hang on the wall;*
> *I'll throw them all into the bargain*
> *If you'll marry my daughter at all.*

Signs of desperation there from a father or mother, but surely they should know that 'God never shuts one door but he opens another', and Heaven knows, the daughter was hardly as bad as the woman who visited Hell in the song that went, in part:

> *There were two little divils a playin' football*
> *Right fol, right fol titty fol day*
> *There were two little divils a playin' football*
> *So she upped with her stick and she scattered them all …*

So, if a family is 'hot and full', 'comfortable', 'with the grass of a goat and a cow', let them not 'strunt' (sulk) if 'gompans' (small amounts) of trouble come their way, for that would be 'flying in God's face' (tempting Providence).

'Wirrasthrua' is a word that survives the passing of the 'keeners'. It is a term of pity concerned with the Mother of Sorrows – '*Muire is trua*' – It's a pity, Mary.

'Stations' exist in parts of the countryside still. Mass was once celebrated in all houses in a parish, and the householder put up a meal for the celebrant. There was great rivalry between households, and the man that came best out of it all was the priest. Small wonder there was rivalry if the report of William Carleton of Prillisk, Co. Tyrone, in his *Amusing Irish Tales* is true. In his story 'Father Philemy' or 'The Holding of the Stations', he describes the scene in the small parish church on Sunday when the announcements are being read out. Picture it yourselves – a scent of burning candles, a multicoloured beam of sun entering from the stained glass window and resting above the altar. Small boys, red soutaned and white surpliced, fiddling with the lace on their sleeves.

Mass over – and all the time in the world to spare:

> '*On Monday, in Jack Gallagher's of Corraghnamoddagh.*
> Are you there, Jack?'
> 'To the fore, yer reverence.'
> 'Why, then, Jack, there's something ominous – something auspicious – to happen or we wouldn't have you

here; for it's very seldom that you make part or parcel of
the *present* congregation; seldom are you here, Jack, it
must be confessed: however, you know the old classical
proverb, or if *you* don't, *I* do, which will answer just as
well – *Non semper ridit Apollo* – it's not every day *Manus*
kills a bullock; so as you *are* here, be prepared for us on
Monday.'

'Never fear, yer reverence, never fear; I think you
ought to know that the grazin' at Corraghnamoddagh's
not bad.'

'To do you justice, Jack, the mutton was always good
with you, only if you would get it better killed, it would
be an improvement.'

'Very well, yer reverence, I'll do it.'

'*On Tuesday, in Peter Murtagh's, of the Crooked Com-
mons.* Are you there, Peter?'

'Here, yer reverence.'

'Indeed, Peter, I might know you are here; and I wish
that a great many of *my* flock would take example by you:
if they did, I wouldn't be so far behind in getting my *dues*.
Well, Peter, I suppose you know that this is Michaelmas?'

'So fat, yer reverence, that they're not able to wag; but,
anyway, Katty has them marked for you – two fine young
craythurs, only last year's fowl, and the ducks isn't a taste
behind them – she's crammin' them this month past.'

'I believe you, Peter, and I would take your word for
more than the condition of the geese – remember me to
Katty, Peter ... *On Wednesday, in Parrah More Slevin's of
Mullaghfadh.* Are you there, Parrah More?' – No answer.
'Parrah More Slevin?' – Silence. 'Parrah More Slevin of
Mullaghfadh?' – No reply. 'Dan Fagan?'

'Present, sir.'

'Do you know what keeps that reprobate from Mass?'

'I believe he's takin' advantage, sir, of the frast, to get
in his praties today, in respect of the bad footin', sir, for
the horses in the bog when there's not a frast. Anyhow,
betune that and a bit of a sore head that he got, yer

reverence, on Thursday last in takin' part wid the O'Scallaghans agin the Bradys. I believe he had to stay away
today.'

'On the Sabbath day too, without my leave! Well, tell
him from me that I'll make an example of him to the
whole parish, if he doesn't attend Mass better. Will the
Bradys and the O'Scallaghans never be done with their
quarrelling? I protest, if they don't live like Christians, I'll
read them out from the altar. Will you tell Parrah More
that I'll hold a station in his house next Wednesday?'

'I will, sir; I will, yer reverence.'

'*On Thursday, in Phaddhy Sheemus Phaddhy's of the Es-
ker*. Are you there, Phaddhy?'

'Wid the help of God, I'm here, sir.'

'Well, Phaddhy, how is yer son, Briney, that's at the
Latin? I hope he's coming on well at it.'

'Why, sir, he's not more nor a year and a half at it yet,
and he's got more books almost nor he can carry – he'll
break me buying books for him.'

'Well, that's a good sign, Phaddhy, but why don't you
bring him to me till I examine him?'

'Well, never a one of me can get him to go, sir, he's so
much afeard of your reverence.'

Well, Phaddhy, we were once modest and bashful
ourselves, and I'm glad to hear that he's afraid of his cler-
gy; but let him be prepared for me on Thursday, and maybe I'll let him know something he never heard before; I'll
give him a Maynooth touch.'

'Do you hear that, Briney?' said the father, aside, to
the son, who knelt at his knee. 'Ye must give up yer hurl-
ing and idling now, you see. Thank yer reverence, thank
you, docthor.'

'*On Friday, in Barny O'Darby's*, alias *Barny Butter's*. Are
you there, Barny?'

'All that's left of me is here, sir.'

'Well, Barny, how is the butter trade this season?'

'It's a little on the rise now, sir; in a month or so I'm

expecting it will be brisk enough; *Borey*, sir, is doing that much for us, anyway.'

'Aye, and Barny, he'll do more than that for us; God prosper *him* at all events – I only hope the time's coming, Barny, when everyone will be able to eat his own butter and his own beef, too.'

'God send it, sir.'

'Well, Barny, I didn't hear from your brother, Ned, these two or three months; what has become of him?'

'Ah, yer reverence, Pentland done him up.'

'What, the gauger?'

'He did, the thief; but maybe he'll sup sorrow for it afore he's much oulder.'

'And who do you think informed, Barny?'

'Oh, I only wish I knew that, sir.'

'I wish *I* knew it; and if I thought any miscreant here would become an *informer*, I'd make an example of him. Well, Barny, on Friday next; but I suppose Ned has a drop still – eh, Barny?'

'Why, sir, we'll apt to have something stronger nor wather, anyhow.'

'Very well, Barny; your family was always a dacent and spirited family, I'll say that for them; but tell me, Barny, did you begin to dam the river yet? I think the trouts and eels are running by this time.'

'The creels are made, yer reverence, though we did not set them yet; but on Tuesday night, sir, wid the help of God, we'll be ready.'

'You can *corn* the trouts, Barny, and the eels too; but should you catch nothing, go to Pat Hartigan, Captain Sloethorn's gamekeeper, and if you tell him it's for me, he'll drag you a batch out of the fish-pond.'

'Ah, then, your reverence, it's 'imself that'll do that wid a heart an' a half.'

An 'unhandy' (awkward) Longford man 'hasn't hands on him to bless himself'.

'As useless as a nun's pap' – a logical if unkind comparison.

An uncle of Padraic Colum married an Anne MacNamee and the couple were invited to an ordination breakfast where they were very tense because they were not used to going to table, especially with priests.

The newly-ordained priest sensed the tension and the unease and, to break the ice, he said to Anne: 'You're a fine looking woman, Anne. You must have been extremely good-looking when you were young. I wonder why you ever took Hugh (her husband)?' Anne replied: 'God's truth, father, and you're a young priest, but that's the truest word you'll ever say. I was indeed good-looking. I had lots of boyfriends. I even had officers out of Longford out here after me.'

This was too much for Hugh who chipped in, 'Faith, then you had, but they were sanitary officers telling you to clean yourself!'

Let us finish this section, loosely based on things religious, with a saying that comes from the obligation to have a certain number in a church before Benediction can be given. The expression is used concerning any event – meeting, match or fair:

'There wasn't enough at it for Benediction.'

Munster

A FELLOW was anxious that the girl he dated should not know about his bad sight, so he stuck a pin in a tree that he walked her past later. As he approached the tree, he said to the girl, 'Do you see the pin stuck in that tree?'

'No,' replied the girl.

Moving over to remove the pin for her, the fellow fell over a cow.

'Did you ever see such a stupid place to leave a bike?' he said.

I tell this story here because it is with great trepidation that I face the task of relating sayings and expressions of Munster. Even with a pin stuck in every branch of the rich flowering tree of Munster dialect, a Midlander must fall and stumble as he tries to grapple with the accent and the idiom. He hasn't 'a snowball's chance in Hell' of conveying on paper the marvellously descriptive language of the southerners.

A 'noggin' is elsewhere a word for head, but in Clare, the Burren Country – called the largest rockery in the world – a 'noggin' is a small plate or dish. 'Drink that what's put in your noggin and you'll get more while ago when you drink what's that.' The remark to a finicky child is awesome in its construction. If the child did not say grace before its meal, it would be told: 'You started dinner like a fox.' (A fox once caught a hen by the neck and was about to settle in a copse to eat it when the hen told it to thank God for its meal. The fox opened its mouth to say grace, and the hen escaped, so Reynard vowed never to say grace again.)

'You'll scratch a beggarman's back yet' warns that one

will be poor some day. It is said in the same circumstances as 'You'll follow the crow for that some day' – if something, particularly food, is wasted.

An 'angishore' (*ainciseoir*) is a miserable wretch.

An 'American Wake' is a farewell party for intending emigrants.

A 'drop in the ocean' describes this 'scratching the sod' or minute sample of a vast amount of sayings.

The very sayings themselves have a name in Clare. 'He was full of old nohawns' means that he had a store or a vast amount of sayings. Some Clare people have a habit of adding the word 'That's' to every statement they make. A father and his daughter, Bridgie, and a third party are involved in the following conversation:

Father (at dance): 'That's Bridgie. That's you can dance her but no wheelin'. That's you don't wrong her.'

Some time later, the father's conversation to the swain goes: 'That's poor Bridgie. That's she's pregnant. That's how you did her wrong, you bastard.'

The accused happens to have an injured wrist at the time, and his answer is: 'That's how could I do it with my hand in a sling?'

Clare people gave portions of any pig they killed to their friends. An unpopular farmer offered portions to his neighbours but they refused. He told how he was disturbed:

'That's how Mary and me were dividing up the pig. That's where nobody would take the heart. That's where nobody would take the liver. That's where nobody would even take the drisheens (puddings). That's how I was woeful put out until Mary said, "Let them, John Joe. We may have no friends, but we have the whole of the old pig anyway".'

In the lovely St Brigid's where a clear spring comes trickling down stone slabs, the only graffiti asks for prayer. High above, the monument of the O'Brien tomb and the larger monument built by his tenants impose themselves on the rise surrounding Daigh Bhrighde where people came from as far away as the Aran Islands on *Satharn Chromdubh*, the day before the last Sunday of July. There they could look over the rare beauty of the Burren, indulge in all sorts of merrymaking between visits to the well for prayer, and talk 'the length and breadth of the day' until night came with its attendant temptations.

Mickey the Mate was a butcher in this area. A stonemason and a painter were both called 'Doctor' for some reason, and when they were introduced as such to a genuine doctor, he was heard to remark of their unkempt appearance, 'What's the profession coming to at all?'

A fine Clare fiddler disliked the '*bodhrán*' (type of tambourine made of goat skin). He declared that the instrument was 'a crude imitation of an ass' arse.'

'There's a dool on me for the jam' – I have a craving for jam. This is used particularly of women who develop longings for certain foodstuffs during pregnancy.

When the weather was very bad in July, a Clareman blamed the Department of Agriculture's scheme when they built glasshouses all over Connemara. His reasoning was: 'Them glasshouses are using up all the sun.'

Tales are told in Clare 'cuarding houses' or '*céilí* houses' – houses where neighbours meet to have a bit of *craic* – of landlords who bestowed favours on tenants who persuaded their daughters to 'be generous' with the gentry. A visitor remarked to a woman some generations after, that her farm of land appeared to be much smaller than that of her neighbours. She was kneading dough at the time and didn't look up as she cynically explained: 'My mother didn't lift her skirts up at the big house.' It is of this area that the story is told of the farmer who saw his daughter being generous to the landlord on a slab of cold Clare stone which had evidence of the passing of cattle upon it. The farmer chastised the daughter saying, 'Biddy, will you rise your buttocks and don't let the muck on the gentleman's ... and the same to you, sir!'

'He had sheroose on him' – he was envious. Neither spelling nor explanation is clear.

An afflicted father of a bride told his new son-in-law at the reception: 'You take your crowd into one room and I'll take mine into another.'

A man sold mackerel on the pier at Liscannor. A prospective customer rooted around the box of fish for the biggest one, until reprimanded by the vendor, 'Is it a shark you want for your tuppence?'

'Be off out of that' – go away.

'Say a *paidirín* (pronounced *podoreen*) for me – say the rosary for me.

'Lord, but you have a sight of *clábar* on you' – you have an amount of mud on you.

'The Seven Curses of Quilty on you!'

And before they start falling upon me, I'm going to 'Skedaddle' (run quickly) away towards Luach.

Clare people who wished to put the '*mí-ádh*' (pronounced *meeawe* – '*mírath*': bad luck) on an enemy, stuck a '*maide*' (stick) in his field and rammed a 'lock' (lump) of butter on the stick. As the butter melted and went bad, ill-luck came to the enemy. A man was 'brought to law' (prosecuted) about such an incident.

'The churn didn't come right' – no butter came from it.

'She was making the churn' – she was churning.

The old custom by which a visitor to a house took a hand in the churning was observed strictly in Clare. If it 'went clean out of a man's head' and he left without doing a 'drass' of the churn, he was likely to be called back to oblige. Known as a 'brash' in Donegal, the 'drass' only involved giving the churn three turns or 'dashes' depending on the type of churn in use. It was a sure way of buttering up the woman of the house!

Clare was a 'Leath-Gaeltacht' – a half Irish-speaking area – but traditional Irish music was kept better than the tongue and, 'as sure as God made little apples', Tulla, Doolin and Kilfenora boasted some of the country's finest traditional musicians.

'Between the jigs and the reels, your man got away' – because of a number of circumstances, he escaped.

A man that married at a late stage of life was '*gan mheabhair roimh a bháis*' – without sense before death – as he demonstrated by getting married at that age in the first place.

That '*cnuas*' (store) of Irish is as old as the hills, and the hills of Clare must be 'as old as Methuselah's cat'.

A 'caish' is a '*banbh*' or a young pig. '*Lioscáns*' were, in hand-harvesting days, the ears of corn left in a field after stooking. A 'cool' is a roll of butter. 'Doorshey daurshey' is 'baloney' or something known to be untrue.

'What the pooka writes, he can read as well!' (The mythical fiend frequented the countryside around 'Hollentide', 'Halloween', 'Hallow-Eve' – on 31 October.) If a person suddenly produces a missing article, and is suspected of stealing and hiding it, the above is said of him.

'Don't be there till you're back again,' requires haste of somebody going on an errand.

A poor person 'hasn't two ha'pennies to rattle together' or 'hasn't as much as would jingle on a gravestone'.

'He'd do a Blackbird on a plate' does not allude to any more extravagant a claim than dancing to a particular tune!

If a man stays too long visiting, he 'would wait for the christening if he went to a wedding' although he might have 'a way with him' and have everybody 'in stitches' or 'splitting their sides' laughing.

'Take a hoult of yourself now' is said to somebody who is getting upset.

'Don't shake hands with the devil until you meet him.' This saying is common in many places. I heard of its being said to a woman who was being wheeled into an operating theatre. She was more philosophical than the speaker was tactful and she replied, 'If I meet him itself, can't I brush past him?' A sick person has 'a dose of the Dundalks', for some unknown reason.

Limerick wit is evident in the man's answer to the girl that shouts, 'Hey, duckie, any chance of your washin'?'

'No fear. You'd eat the soap!'

A pair 'doing a line' or 'great' (courting) are 'tackin''. If this state existed for some time, it would be said: 'They were tackin' for so long, he wore into a cape and bonnet.'

A well-dressed lady is 'laid out like an altar', but a badly-dressed lady is a 'feck for the Junction' or a 'Holy Show'.

A Limerick woman was heard to remark: 'As true as the Blessed Virgin died on the altar, she's pregnant.'

'Swan skin' was a type of flannel, a 'slugabed' is a lazy lout, and a 'pulloge' is a cache of apples robbed from an orchard.

🌳🌳🌳🌳🌳🌳🌳🌳

A freshly-cut straw could be made into a crude musical instrument called a '*geocán*' in most country places. Limerick people called this a 'jokawn'. It was even more humble than the 'trump' or 'Jew's Harp'.

'Look at your coat all in *giobals* (rags).' That would be said to a 'flipper', a ragged man. A tiny insect covered in a frothy liquid sometimes settles on a '*tráithnín*' (blade of grass). This is 'cuckoo-spit'.

Full-length mirrors in stores are called 'body-glasses'.

If a fellow were asked a question and gave a very wrong answer, he would be told: 'You're not within an ass' roar of it.' And off the ashamed fellow would go, 'with his tail be-tween his legs' or 'without an inch of tail'. By the way, the same fellow was so mean that 'he'd grow a boil on the back of his neck rather than buy a stud'.

Tipperary and Waterford

> ...When queenly Slievenamon puts her verdant
> vesture on
> And smiles to hear the news the breezes bring;
> When the sun begins to glance on the rivulets
> that dance,
> Ah, sweet is Tipperary in the spring.

It always amazes me how one can remember lines learned in one's very tender years, while stanzas studied for hours later in life have all gone. Sayings stick in the mind too. From the time of the Rural Electrification scheme I remember a 'cant' in Tipperary that went: 'They're all lit up – like Shinrone!'

Tipperary people, be they 'as solid as the rock of Cashel' or only 'knee high to a grasshopper', are 'wise out' (intelligent). They talk and make noise 'like bluebottles in a butter-box' and say things like the following:

'Be the holy man.'

'Be the powers.'

'Be the hokey.'

''Pon me soul.'

They call rabbits 'underground mutton'. Noses they call 'conks'. Their house is a 'cage' and a car's self-starter is a 'commencer'. They are all words cooked up by witty people to suit society, but older sayings like 'He's only a long string of misery' and 'He'd eat cabbage till the cows come home' are still heard.

A child hanging out of its mother in a sulk is 'sucking after her', and courting a Clonmel girl is 'stalking a moll'. An old sixpence or 'tanner' was a 'sprazzi' there, and money took on an Eastern title: 'denarii'.

Having 'drawn his dole' at a factory (modern), a Tipperary man will 'away home to the hen' who might be so pretty that 'she'd make a cat turn backwards'. 'You'd stand to look at her', in fact. Then again, she might 'rub you up the wrong way', 'come down on you like a ton of bricks', 'keep you tied to her apron stings' and 'as sober as a nun on Good Friday'. She might even 'make St Peter swear'.

'God made enough for the needy but not for the greedy.'

'I didn't know where to put my face' – I was ashamed. This is the same as: 'I wished the ground would open up and swallow me.'

'I'll bring that fellow to the cleaners; I'll take him for every penny he has' – I'll get all his money out of him.

'Take the bockle out of that rope' – take the knot out of it.

'Give over your baking (meaning using the beak, or *bake* as it is pronounced) – stop talking.

'You're a right go by the road' – you're no good.

'Hand me the smalkera (wooden spoon).'

'He paid on the nail (promptly).'

'He was doing a Rattle-the-Hasp around the haggard.' The hasp was the latch of the door which was often taken down for dancing upon, especially if it was a half-door. A dance soon was called the 'Rattle-the-Hasp' and the sentence describes a man who was edgy and flying around the farm-yard. He might have been 'going from Billy to Jack' if there were other men there. (Hopping from one to the other, more often said of a flirty girl.)

Ah yes, Tipperary has 'the gift of the gab' all right – and if you don't believe me, grab Charles Kickham's *Knocknagow* and read of Matt the Thresher and all those wonderful people. I wouldn't dream of dwelling any longer in a county that has such a book 'trotting out' all its fine sayings and expressions.

But hurry! The Knockmealdowns beckon to the Galtees, so away with us down by Clogheen and across the 'V' to Lismore where King John's son ate too much salmon. We'll take his trail to Waterford where he broke out in a rash and where his regal father built a leper hospital, thinking his son to have the dreaded disease. He must have done some 'quare *cnáimhseáil-ing*' (complaining) when he found out that the young fellow 'hadn't anything more wrong with him than Kilfarassy'.

A peculiar Waterford expression is: 'Me and the lack are going to the pictures', and the spelling of 'lack' cannot be ascertained nor can its origin, but it is akin to Dublin's 'mot', and means the girlfriend.

'What is wrong with you at all, at all?'; 'What in the wide world is wrong with you?' – What on earth is wrong with you?

'It was all his trouble to help' – he wanted very much to assist.

'There's a stepmother's breath in the day'; 'There's a bite in it'; 'There's a thin bit of a wind blowing'; 'There's a cut in the wind that would go through you' – as you may have gathered already, it was 'a skinnin' cold day'.

'I saw her as often as twins have toes' or 'as often as twins have fingers and toes'. This is more often used without the added advantage of twins.

'I have a *bonnleac* that's killing me' – I have a callus that's hurting me.

'He's like a *fear bréige* (scarecrow)' – he's not looking well, not dressed well.

'I think I'll hain the mill field' – I think I'll let the mill field into meadow.

'It's about as watertight as a *ciséan* (basket).'

Unsuspecting people might think that a 'lusmore' was an inhabitant of the eminent town of the Decies. Far from it! It is the name of the flower, foxglove, the '*méaracáin 'a sí*' or 'fairies' thimble' – how beautifully descriptive!

Potatoes mashed with butter are 'pandy', here as in many other counties.

Sounding like 'philibeen', *pilibín* is a common word for the bird known as the plover.

If a Waterford man is ordained, he is 'priested'. If he doesn't 'go the course' in the seminary, he leaves to become what was once spoken of only in whispers around Ireland – a spoiled priest.

'He paid rack-rent' – he paid a very high rent. If landlords imposed this on their tenants, they were likely to finish up one fine day 'with their eye in a sling'. Many of the same landlords had 'a rag on every bush' down around Waterford – they had a number of girlfriends – perhaps in the hostelries in the city where inhabitants were permitted by charter to distil '*uisce beatha*' (water of life – whiskey).

King John gave this city its first charter which granted it and the harbour to the citizens. He founded its Corporation in 1205 and 'it never looked back since' – it flourished.

We heard earlier of Diarmuid Mac Murrough giving the Rock of Dunamase with Aoife as a dowry. Well, it was in the tower of Waterford that the wedding took place. He must have 'made a mint' (made plenty of money) out of the Rock, for there soon *was* a mint in the Tower.

'When all fruit fails, welcome haws' – anything is welcome if one has nothing.

'Galloping horses won't see the mark' – the mark is hardly noticeable.

'She's as sound as a bell' – she's healthy.

'It's about as clear as ditch water' – it's not at all clear.

'There's a sight of piocks on the potatoes' – there are many sprouts on them.

But let's get out of here at a 'sling-trot' – jogging smartly. There's 'a share of' (many) people heading for Tramore for the races, and the Doneraile Walk will be like Finaghy field tonight with all the 'sergeants' (pint stout bottles) that will be lying about.

Cork and Kerry

It's really only to tease them that I throw them together in this section. They claim undying enmity to each other. They say that they hate each other's guts but I suspect that, secretly, they are very fond of each other. They have reason to be too, for both Cork and Kerry possess an enviable tradition of prowess in physical and intellectual endeavours.

An old train once had a collision with a steamroller – and came off best – but sure, all Cork puffers do! I only heard of one Corkman who did not get what he wanted. He had seven girls in the family and dearly wanted a son. Well, his wife was 'preggers' (a refined Cork expression!) again and an old Coal Quay lady kept inquiring about the outcome, until she was informed that an eighth daughter had arrived. The advice she gave the father was: 'Next time you go about your little bit of business again, like, put on your hat and face Shandon.'

Please try to recall the Cork accent when reading these sayings and expressions for it is the lilt that sings through a couple of octaves as they speak that makes the Cork sayings so attractive. My biggest problem was to get them to slow down so that I could get even the 'gist' of what they said. They greet you with something like: 'What yer, aul sthock, Deabhalta Mouth the water.' That's the way they 'hold you and eat you' – welcome you.

The half-crown side and the shillin'-side of 'Pana' are relics of the days when a noble profession was practised for small remuneration. The only commerce practised on the street now is newspaper selling, and a shout of 'Eee-c-ooooo' from an *Echo* Boy seems to last until he gets a customer.

Of a 'poor *cuirliún*' (curlew, a simple lad is called thus in many parts), they say, 'It would be an ease to us if someone took him off our hands.' A 'poor crill' is another form.

'Oh, he's all his Daddy's' or 'He's me Dazer' – he's marvellous.

'How is himself? Is he working?'
'Working, is it? He wouldn't sleep the same house as a

shovel standing up.'

Another complaint about the husband went. 'With the weight of him and the hate (heat) of him and the smell of stale porter off his bret (breath), I thinks the dawn will never break.'

'Oh Ma, am I tidy! I'm off to have a scounge with Johnny Die.' Nicknames are ten-a-penny in Cork. Even a bishop was known as 'Danny Boy'. This reverend gentleman conversed with a Corkwoman:

'How are things?'

'Yesha, flyin'. Johnny is in Dunlops', Jimmy is off the dole and Katie is in the family way.'

The bishop replied, 'When she's my age, she'll be in everybody's way.'

Another bishop insisted on the one full meal and two 'coalitions' (collations) per day during Lent. He did allow a cup of tea and a biscuit at suppertime, however. A firm of confectioners brought out a gigantic biscuit which was immediately dubbed a 'Dodger'.

Of a family called 'Hoare', it was said: 'That street has the young hoores running all over it.'

A Corkman on a date 'has a jag'. A more permanent arrangement is known as 'square-pushing'. The girl is a 'pusher'. This term is not used in the derogatory sense.

A goalie playing with 'The Bars' (St Finbarr's) let four or five *sliotar*s past him before a selector roared, 'Come out of it before the score is bigger than the attendance!'

'Backs to the wall, lads, here's the Bandon bus.' The explanation that I heard for this common Cork saying will not be given here – especially when I think of the Cork threat, 'I'll put your two eyes into one!'

The well-off people of Cork are 'pound noteish'. A tall man is 'like the top of a Cork road' in Youghal, and a stubborn child might declare, 'I'll ate no bite at all' if he gets 'drisheens' (black puddings) again for his dinner.

The Christian Brothers' School is known as 'Christians', and it sounds peculiar to a stranger to hear, 'You'll know we're Christians by the colour of our *geansaí*s (jerseys)'.

'I was run in from walking up and down, boyya,' complained a nurse to her boyfriend. The unsympathetic reply came:

'And why didn't you walk sideways, girlea?'

'Ask me arm, kiss me toe, strike me now with the child in me arms' – a type of a general purpose expression.

'Get it honest if you can but have it anyhow' – hardly a typical piece of Cork advice, but a typical Cork rhyme goes:

> 'Aroo from Cork?' – 'I am, aroo?'
> 'D'ya ate potatoes? – 'Begor, I do.'
> 'What way d'ya ate 'em?' – 'Skin an' all.'
> 'D'ya not peel 'em?' – 'Yerra, Christ, no, not at all!'

A caller for Mickey heard Mickey being paged within the house: 'Hey, Mickey, come down upstairs.'

'Here's a *tomhaisín* (pronounced 'towsheen') of snuff for you.'

'I had it on the tip of my tongue' – I had the word required but I cannot now remember it.

'He was a strong farmer. He never shook the hand of a bank manager.'

A street rhyme that Cork children use goes something like:

> *Johnny up a donkey,*
> *Johnny up a pole;*
> *Johnny up a donkey, three years old.*

St Multose is said to have been refused help by natives of Kinsale when he tried to heave a stone onto the church he was building. A stranger helped him and only strangers do well in Kinsale since that day. 'Yerra, who d'ye think ye're coddin'?'

Casting eyes down demurely at an approaching male is uncommon nowadays, yet a Cork girl remarked in conversation, 'Next time I sees him, I brushes me buttons.'

Somebody that's 'mockia like' is stuck-up or affected.

Ballyhooley, location of many a faction fight in olden times, passes this tradition into its dialect. If a woman gives her son 'the length and breadth of her tongue' – a telling-off – that is 'Ballyhooley'. Everybody the world over knows about the word 'Blarney'. Here's an example of another Cork trait – a delight in taking a rise out of a fellow, especially in the matter of drink:

Tim Pat comes into the bar and commences an argument with the publican about a score in a certain match. Now, Tim Pat knows the winning margin was three points but he argues with the publican that it was five points. The argument is unresolved when Tim Pat moves to the other end of the counter in the busy bar and tells the barman that 'the boss' told him he could have three pints of porter on the house (free). The barman stares in disbelief until Tim Pat shouts down to the publican, 'Wasn't it three "pints" you said?' 'Yes,' replies the publican. 'There y'are now,' says Tim Pat to the barman and he gets his three pints.

Well, 'a lala', that's 'the holy all of it' from the 'Holy Ground', so I leave you with a Cork farewell:

'Good luck, boyya, keep in by the wall and mind the buses.'

You know, the trouble with Kerry sayings is that a stranger cannot distinguish between established sayings and 'span new' ones: 'His Adam's apple hung out like a doorknob', for instance.

'St Patrick was never in Kerry,' taunt the Corkmen.

'How could he when the Cork crowd stole his ass?' comes the quick retort. The Kerryman takes the initiative:

'We gave you the Blackwater (river).'

'It couldn't wait to get out of Kerry.'

John B. Keane is the master of the Kerry descriptive saying. An ardent lover states: 'Give me a fair slip and a long course and there's no hare I won't turn.' His advice to a 'wishy-washy' courtier was 'Blasth you, wouldn't you make a drive at her and take her in your arms and swear your honest love for her and hould her for a minute by the butt of the ear with them two black fangs of yours? A kettle was never boiled without fire and a woman was never won by wishing.'

'She looks a bit long in the tooth for me'; 'She's getting on a bit' – she's getting old. 'Use a bit of coaxiorum on her' – coax her. What age would she be without giving her age away? She's like a cormorant going to the bog, can't give up her momentum, is fluthered' – how inadequate is the word 'intoxicated' by comparison!

Back from his honeymoon, a Kerryman said, 'I never thought you could have so much fun without laughing'. Another newly-wed slept in his own home and his father called him for the milking as usual in the morning. He stayed on in bed with his new wife, however. The farmer kept calling and knocking at the door.

At last, the young man answered his father: 'Take away me clothes and burn them, father. I'm gettin' up no more.'

'She finished her spiel'; 'She put a sock in it'; 'She done with her spake' – she stopped talking.

Ready wit? During Writers' Week a barrel of porter (a tierce) fell off a lorry and burst on the street. The remark from a local? – 'Ink for Writers' Week!'

'As black as a famine spud' is a fine Kerry saying.

'Rail-tail' is twist tobacco.

Telling lies is tolerated to a certain extent but if a man goes too far with it they say: 'There's lies and lies in it.'

A *sciollán* is a piece of potato cut to leave one sprout or 'eye' for growing. A 'quin' is a beam that keeps plough chains separated to avoid their chaffing the horses. The '*gligín*' or incessant talker of nonsense is less welcome than the '*geocach*' who is lazy but likable. The Irish '*cró*' is still used for a cow shed, and a 'cow's lick' is a child's hair swept across and upwards on its brow. A 'caffler' is cheeky and a 'birragh' is an apparatus to prevent a young animal from sucking its mother.

'Buds' or 'Budderys' derived form *'bodaire'* or *'bodach'* (uncouth lout) are the people of the Kerry countryside that mingle with the stranger in the watering place of Ballybunion.

'Are you out lookin' at the mornin'?' – I received that greeting in Kerry. 'Come in here and apply your arse to the seat of the stool,' the speaker went on. 'I was heavy drunk last night,' he admitted. He had a story of being 'caught between two stools' – caught between two factions. 'I'm the ham in the "sangwidge",' he said.

'Give us a pint of loose porter. May you live as long as you want and never want as long as you live.'

'If you want praise, die, but if you want blame, marry.'

'Wouldn't you have taken a lease of his life, and there he is now, dead as a doornail.'

'Will you take a fiver for that old coat?'

'Would a cat take milk?'; 'Would I what?' – of course I would.

'Get shut of that one. She's roarin' and beakin' about the house like a suck-calf after losing its mother.'

'Ah, the light of heaven on you!'

'Yerra, whisht your *plámás'* – stop playing up to me with sweet words.

I wonder do the people of Fenit know that they gave a saying to the pig trade. When maize was imported from America to be mixed with buttermilk for pig-feeding, farmers said, 'If you get more for a fat pig than you paid for a ton of maize at Fenit Pier, then it pays to fatten pigs'.

Amusing Bulls, Anecdotes and Original Expressions

FAR FROM being an extinct species, the Irish bull regularly snorts its way into conversations. As recently as 1984, a Department of Justice official was quoted as saying: 'If Mr X was still employed in the prison service, he would be sacked.'

Speaking of a depleted library in a certain institution, a member said: 'What's in it is all taken away.'

At a speechmaking competition, a competitor began: 'Before I speak, I want to say a few words.' A delighted winner of the competition said, 'I'm first at last; I was always behind before.'

A man visited Knock shrine for the first time in twenty years. He noted vast improvements – such as the small church replaced by a huge basilica. Telling about his experience, he said: 'I swear if I was blindfolded I'd have thought I was in Rome.'

Flattery about appearance can bring about remarkable observations:

'You look as if you're only twenty.'

'I'm every day of thirty-two.'

'I can see that but you only look twenty.'

'Is this the house where the dead man lives?' asks an intending sympathiser. 'It is,' he is told, 'but he (the deceased) will be coming to the church at seven o'clock.'

'Where were you rushing to when I saw you going to work this morning?'

A timber-merchant displays a beam of the finest mahogany to a customer and says: 'You won't find the likes of that growing on trees.'

A tourist asks directions from a countryman who replies: 'You know, I don't think you can get to there from here.'

A chat-show host was telling television viewers about that evening's guests. 'We will be discussing a fatal drug,' he said, 'and I'll be talking to a victim.'

About to bring her husband's jacket to the dry-cleaners', a lady found a receipt for a double room in a pocket. When she questioned him later, he defended himself saying, 'I must have stayed there twice.'

'She had a bottom lip you could trip over.'

'She was as cross as a wet hen.'

'He would take the eye out of your head and tell you you were better-looking without it.'

'Jack crashed the car.'

'Is it badly smashed?'

'Badly smashed! The bleedin' headlights are in the boot!'

> *A good coffee should be drunk*
> *Black as the Earl of Hell's boot,*
> *Hot as his hearth,*
> *But sweet as love.*

'Careless! He would leave a squirrel minding nuts.'

'I'm fifty years a Pioneer (member of a temperance movement.' – 'Please God you'll live to break it.'

A funeral cortège inched its way up steep Shandon Street in Cork in the old days of horse-drawn hearses. The horse slipped, the coffin fell out and the lid came off, leaving the corpse exposed. A 'shawlie' crossed herself and said, 'Jaysus, he's kilt!'

Comedian Noel Purcell had an amusing way of telling a priest that he was prepared to die: 'Tell the gaffer that Purcell is ready when he is.'

'They say she can dance.' – 'Dance! She taught St Vitus!'

Of a woman with big feet, it was said: 'She would be grand if there wasn't so much of her on the ground.'

An ageing chauvinist was boasting about alleged affairs with women. His companion remarked, with contempt: 'You're like an old dog chasing a bicycle; if you caught it, you couldn't ride it.'

'He's a solid farmer with a bull in the field, a pump in the yard and a son in Maynooth.'

'Aren't we wintering well? Do you think we will see the swallows?'

'That fellow would hear a midge landing on a leaf a mile away.'

'You should mind that cold, Mary.' – 'Why should I? Sure I want to get rid of it.'

'That fellow is as idle as the left hand of a *bodhrán* player.'

'He gave her a big sloppy kiss that would water a horse.'

'Look at the head of that fellow and the price of turnips.

Some coarse, yet amusing utterances have been spoken about love and pregnancy.

An Irishman's foreplay is something like, 'Brace yourself, girleen.'

Of a pregnant wife it was said, 'It's no good threshing when the barn is full' and 'It's no use throwing the sheaf up against the barn door'.

Of a pregnant bride it was said, 'They went before the whistle, but isn't it great to have had so much done!'

However, the wisest witticism on the subject must surely be: 'If you're in love with a manure heap, you'll find a dry straw.'

A certain publican was noted for putting very little between the bread slices of his sandwiches. A customer said, 'That fellow is so mean he slices the Easy-singles.'

In Cavan, they 'would make the tea when you go home' (are very mean) and they 'have their dinner out of a drawer'. A Cavan woman asked a visitor how he would like his egg boiled. He an-swered, 'With another.' 'Very well,' she said, 'I'll boil it with my own.'

Of a country-and-western singer whose songs were mainly about place-names, it was said: 'He's the musical wing of the Ordnance Survey.'

'She was screaming like a long-tailed cat in a room full of rocking chairs.'

Of a boy fishing, a man asked, 'Are you fishing, little boy?' The smart lad answered, 'No! I'm drowning maggots'.

It was known that a reprobate student doctor was related to a distinguished surgeon. A colleague asked, 'What are you to Professor X?' The reprobate replied, 'An embarrassment'.

'You would need to keep the legs of the bed in your boots in that lodging-house.'

'That's so small it wouldn't put a patch on a leprechaun's breeches.'

Of an incessant talker it was said, 'You could get Luxembourg (the radio station) on her!'

'They were scattered all over the place like a nymphomaniac's underclothes.'

'That thing is as useless as an ashtray on a motor-bike.'

'Look at the smile of the hypocrite – like the brass plate on a coffin. With that smile on his face, the barber should give him a shave at half-price.'

'When you look at the west of Ireland, it's easy to see why the wise men came from the East.'

'There are more ways of getting to the top of the tree than by sitting on an acorn.'

'That wind would go through you instead of around you.'

A lady fumbled with the car's gears when the traffic-lights changed to green. The male driver of the car behind criticised her to his wife. 'She's only collecting her wits,' defended the wife. The husband retorted, 'She doesn't have to file them away.'

A drunkard, gambler, fornicator – 'Oh he was a rale right wrong one.'

A thin man – 'I often saw more mate (meat) on a tinker's stick after a row at a fair in Mullingar.'

'It was America at home' – very comfortable.

'Wouldn't you think the moon would come out on a dark night?'

'She fractured her wrist and she's all in plaster.'

'God help the rich; the poor can beg.'

'He's always sucking up to me; sometimes he's so far up my arse I can taste him.'

'Good Luck, What Never'

… Is it the tender tone,
Soft as the stringed harp's moan?

THERE'S NOTHING like a 'blast of a song' and 'one for the road' before parting, and Gerald Griffin's lines from 'Aileen Aroon' pose the question that must be asked if the written word fails to convey the full impact of the charm that abounds in the dialect of the Irish countryside.

As I scan the notebook, scraps of paper, letters and books wherein lies the material from which this book was compiled, and notice how many entries remain unused, unticked – some unrepeatable, I realise that the collection presented forms but a microcosm of the sayings, expressions and anecdotes that gambol on the lips of our people.

It is 'a nice how do you do' that I have to 'dry up' while so many more 'will never see the light of day'. As I say *'Slán is Beannacht'*, 'I'll see you', and 'All the best' I can only say of the rejected ones:

'I could write a book about them.'

MORE INTERESTING BOOKS
FROM MERCIER

'... *Before the Devil Knows You're Dead*'
Irish Blessings, Toasts and Curses

Padraic O'Farrell

Hearing news of a death or marriage, consoling neighbours in sorrow or sharing their joy, looking for a husband or wife, saving turf or going fishing – Irish people had blessings and curses for every occasion.

* *'May you be in heaven an hour before the devil knows you're dead'*

* *'May God give you luck and put a good man in your way, and if he is not good, may the wedding whiskey be drunk at his wake.'*

* *'May today be the first day of the best years of your life.'*

* *'When the road rises to meet you may it slap you in the face.'*

* *'May you be plagued with an itch and no nails to scratch.'*

* *'May the wind always be at your back.'*

The above is just a sample from the blessings and curses collected by Padraic O'Farrell in this book. Luckily many of the old sayings have survived. A few startling new ones have been added too!

Irish Rogues, Rascals and Scoundrels

Padraic O'Farrell

A rogue is a dishonest or unprincipled person – but in a jocular context a rogue is a mischievous child, or a waggish individual. These are dictionary definitions but dictionaries can never define the Irish rogue. This character my well be dishonest or unprincipled. More often, he is a 'likable rogue', that is a rascal and a scoundrel tolerated for his fun and his penchant for taking the harm out of his indiscretions by some redeeming act. Irish facetiousness towards the species may be judged by the parental chastisement: 'You're a right little rascal'.

Our history has thrown up a variety of rogues and scoundrels The likable rogue, the impish rascal, the schemer, the hypo-critical *plámás* and the downright cad – each genre is re-presented in Padraic O'Farrell's collection, including the Sham Squire, Alfie Byrne, Jack Doyle, 'Kruger' and 'Madams of Monto'.

The Wasp in the Mug:
Unforgettable Irish Sayings

Translated by
Gabriel Rosenstock

The wit and wisdom of the Gael are tightly packed in the Irish proverb.

> *Is mó an torann ná an olann*
> *Mar a dúirt an chaora leis an ngabhar a bhí á lomadh.*

> Much cry and little wool
> As the sheep said of the goat being shorn.

***

> *Is sleamhain an lao nach lífidh a mháthair féin í.*

> Slippery the calf that its own mother won't lick!

The Wasp in the Mug is a generous selection of old Irish proverbs like these, newly translated from the Irish by Gabriel Rosenstock, the most prolific poet and translator of his generation. He invites us to savour this collection as a bag of liquorice allsorts – to be dipped into and enjoyed when we feel the urge. But remember: 'Don't keep them all to yourselves. They're for sharing…!'

Irish Blessings, Toasts & Traditions

Edited by
Jason S. Roberts

Often it is said that the Irish are born with the gift of the blarney – and an Irishman can certainly tell a tale like no other. In the rich tradition of Irish lore and legend, tales of fairies with magical powers are the most common as well as the most enjoyable, for when fairies are present there is always the possibility of great fortune or unwitting disaster, not to mention a good story.

This delightful collection brings together the luck and charm of the Irish in a single volume filled with blessings, toasts, old-fashioned customs, sayings, superstitions, jokes, limericks and legends.

Even throughout the Irish countryside today, simple gestures may be seen that are reminiscent of half-remembered rituals. Modern practices of all kinds can be traced back to old customs and traditions, and even old Irish sayings have a familiar ring.

You'll find common remedies for simple ailments such as headache, heartache or freckles – and love spells using herbs and poetry.